Contents

Acknowledgements

This book is dedicated to anyone who has ever felt the clammy grip of fear closing around their heart when a very important file refuses to open. If you've ever lost thousands and thousands of words or a painstakingly constructed spreadsheet or an intricately designed PDF, then my heart goes out to you. Back up your files, kids. Back 'em all up as often as you can.

The patience, love and understanding of my incredible wife Rachael was key to my survival of that awful moment. Without her, I'd have cracked like an egg.

Thanks also to the staff of Zone Content, experts in design and technology and based in Camden, whose IT men tried in vain to retrieve 17,000 words of lbw explanations and historical descriptions of the formative years of the game. They weren't successful, but they fought as if it were their own book that had vanished and they didn't complain when I dried my tears on their mousemats.

I never told my publisher, Charlotte Atyeo, about all of this for two reasons. Firstly, because I didn't want to worry her, and secondly because I hadn't been paid yet. Thankfully, it's all behind us now, eh? Eh? Ok … I'll get me coat… Thanks to Lucy Beevor too, for putting this all together.

Shrimperzone.com, the UK's best Southend United website, were the perfect sounding board for many of the features here. Thanks go to CanveyShrimper, Napster, EastStandBlue, BalmainShrimper, Number 11, Billericay Blue, Southchurch Groyney, Dave and Matt the Shrimp.

Thanks also to Tony Pearson, Toby Fuhrman, Tom Warren, Shaun Nickless, Dan Bourke, James Findlay, Matt Gallagher, Dave Adams, Phil Adams, Mikey Grady, Amy Grady and everyone at The Junction in Tufnell Park.

Thanks, finally, to Steve Brierley, for his invaluable aid in the final stages of proofreading.

Author's Note

As this book is written purely in an effort to make cricket seem simple, you will have to forgive me for referring to every hypothetical person as a 'he'. This is by no means a reflection on my views of gender politics especially as, at the time of writing, the female England cricket side were far more dominant than their male counterparts.

I know that it would be more politically correct to find a way round the problem with words, but I didn't want to end up with a book that read, 'And then the bowler will begin his or her run-up and deliver the ball to the batsman/woman who will try to hit as hard as he or she can.' I think we can all agree that that would have got really tiresome really quickly.

Cricket is a wonderful sport and it doesn't matter whether there's a crossbar on your bicycle or not, it's open to everyone.

Anyway, what are you doing hanging around here debating semantics? There's a wonderful game to discover!

Why you should like cricket

I'm afraid that it is a well-established fact that any introduction to a cricket guide should include a set lexicon of words and phrases. I am therefore obliged, before we even get started on the rules, to chunter on for a number of paragraphs about glorious English summer afternoons at the village green, the gentle thwack of leather on willow, warm beer and vicars on bicycles, small boys with scoreca… Nope … it's no good, I can't do it.

It is a curious phenomenon that cricket, a sport which embraces technology with far more readiness than any other outside of motor racing, is so intrinsically linked with this odd snapshot of what appears to be a BBC costume drama. This isn't to dismiss the cliché entirely, of course. There is, after all, a lot to be said for the warm beer. But it just seems such a shame to focus entirely on a lazy stereotype. We're selling the sport short. Cricket offers so much more.

It has prospered in nations where both football and rugby have failed to hold a beachhead. It is as compelling to the veteran as it is to the newcomer. It has brought people of different, even of conflicting, backgrounds together. There are dressing rooms where Muslims, Hindus, Sikhs and Christians all share locker space. It can be the most charming and honourable of sports, but it can also be brutal, competitive and downright nasty.

There are no quiet village greens in the Indian Premier League, where the fireworks and dancing girls reign supreme, and you're certainly not limited to warm beer at a Test match. Cricket is more inclusive, more exciting and more accessible than ever before. You really couldn't have picked a better time to find this book.

It is a game of such beautiful simplicity and yet it is blessed with layers so complex that it can be anything to anyone. Twenty20 offers the spectator an adrenaline-fuelled, hi-octane explosion of big hits, while the more cerebral Test match is like watching two generals carefully trying to outwit one another, their hopes dependent on the courage and concentration of their men, on the wear and tear of one strip of grass and, of course, on the weather. And yet whatever form of the game you watch, it all comes down to one thing: the ability of a man to hit a ball with a bit of wood.

But few sports are as difficult to understand as cricket. It *is* complicated, but only at the outset. Most naysayers, quite understandably, find it all too confusing. They complain that there are too many numbers, too many weird rules and that it is all too slow. They wonder how anyone can sit through five days and not see a result at the end. I assume, given that you are tentatively flicking through this introduction in a book shop somewhere, that you have always been one of these people. But something has changed, hasn't it? Something has made you look harder and search deeper for the appeal of the game. I applaud you and I hope that you will not be disappointed.

I couldn't, in the confines of these pages, ever hope to do anything more than scrape the surface of this magnificent game. There are better writers and bigger books, but perhaps none that will take you by the hand and guide you through the mess in quite the same way as this one will. There will be no jargon, and no insular codewords or slang will pass by unexplained. This is cricket for the uninitiated, for the brave nomads from other sports wondering what all the fuss is about. This is cricket broken down and put back together, piece by piece. Here you'll discover an easy explanation of that infernal leg-before-wicket issue. You'll know your maidens from your silly mid-off and you'll find out exactly why catches win matches.

People have been playing cricket for over four hundred years and you're just over a hundred pages away from finding out why. So pad up, put on your helmet, adjust your box and grab your bat.

You're next in.

The history of cricket

Cricket is old. Really old. It's older than the great-grandparents of the oldest person you've ever met. It's older than both football and rugby put together. It pre-dates the Spanish Armada and William Shakespeare and, in one form or another, it almost certainly pre-dates the discovery of America. A spring chicken it is not.

As such, even the historians with more time on their hands than me have struggled to find its origins. One widely held theory is that it was developed in the fields of rural England by work-shy shepherds who used their staffs to hit rocks thrown at a target placed behind them. It's a good theory and it makes sense, not least because one olde name for a staff is 'cricce', though that does indicate that in a parallel universe this could be a book about a game called staff-it, or even stick-it. I think I'd have preferred stick-it.

The first written mention of cricket came in 1598 during a legal dispute over land in Guildford. A 59 year old, by the name of John Derrick if you're interested, is recorded as telling the court that he played cricket on the land as a child which means, assuming that he wasn't telling porkies, we can date the sport as far back as about 1548, at least. It wasn't competitive, it wasn't organised, but there it was. Stick-it. Sorry, cricket.

In 1611, some 50 years before the Great Fire of London, two men were prosecuted for daring to play cricket on a Sunday instead of going to church. However, unlike the proto-football matches that were repeatedly banned by monarchs of the day, there isn't any evidence to suggest that the game suffered from the wrath of the authorities. Given that village football matches often ended in serious injury and destruction of property, you can see why cricket might even have been encouraged, provided that it was played in the park and not in the garden near the greenhouse.

After the restoration of the English monarchy and the overthrow of the killjoy Puritans in 1660, cricket began to grow in popularity. For a whole generation of gleeful aristocrats looking for something to do with their leisure time, cricket was a godsend. Not only was it good fun to play, but it was compelling to watch and, like most things, it became even more compelling when you staked half of Daddy's fortune on it. Gambling was one of the key, but not the only, motivating forces in these embryonic days of the sport. Social top bods like Charles Lennox, a grandson of Charles II, captained teams against those led by men like his good friend Sir William Gage. Much merriment ensued, lots of money was won and lost and cricket began to spread around the country.

In 1728, the first rules of cricket were set down on paper. These 'Articles of Agreement' kept the game on the straight and narrow-ish, even when huge stakes of money were being put up for every match. It also made it easier for the men in the far reaches of the Empire to propagate the good word. The British had outposts or colonies in the West Indies, India, South

Africa and down in Australia and New Zealand, so there were plenty of people to teach. It must have been a nervous time for the inhabitants of conquerable nations. Get turned over by the French and you get some decent recipes and the language of love. Get the English and it's cricket and queuing.

The Articles were officially codifed in 1744, but it was 1774 when the first of many amendments were made. You see, cricket in those days wasn't quite the game you might watch now. For starters, all bowling was under-arm, bats were shaped like hockey sticks and wickets only had two stumps. In 1774, the leg-before-wicket (lbw) rule was introduced as well as a crucial clarification on the maximum width of a bat, which you just know was introduced because some bright spark walked out to the crease one day with a bat the size of a trestle table.

By this time, cricket was becoming an established part of British society. Still wildly popular with the upper classes, one of the primary clubs in existence was the White Conduit Club, so-called because they played their games on White Conduit Fields in Islington, London. The only problem they had was that the fields were very public and the gentlemen players were not amused to find the local populace constantly wandering onto the outfield to call them names. In desperation, they turned to one of their players, the bowler Thomas Lord. Lord, despite his name, wasn't an aristocrat, but he was an astute businessman and a very good bowler, hence his professional status within the club. He managed to find an area in north London called Dorset Fields (now Dorset Square) where they could play in peace and it became known as 'Lord's'. That original site wasn't actually the Lord's that we know now though. Another venue was used before they finally arrived in St John's Wood. However, it was at

Dorset Fields where the Marylebone Cricket Club (MCC) was formed in 1787.

The MCC were the guardians of cricket for over 200 years. They looked after the rules, organised the England team and attempted to maintain the spirit of cricket for future generations. Although they have often been criticised and dismissed as introverted and old-fashioned (they refused to admit women as members until 1998), they did successfully guide the sport through some fairly seismic changes.

The 19th century saw the gradual change from under-arm bowling, through round-arm bowling and finally to what we now know to be over-arm bowling. It also saw W. G. Grace, a kind of terrifyingly huge anti-Santa Claus, become the first great cricketing legend after making his debut in 1865. People would travel across the country, on the new-fangled train network, to see him in action. Grace was a phenomenal batsman but also, reportedly, something of a diva. After being bowled first ball in one match he refused to leave the pitch. 'Play on,' he is said to have told the umpire. 'These people have come to see me bat, not you umpire.'

By 1877, the first English touring side was in Australia and, by 1882, their clashes were so avidly followed that a defeat at the Oval in London was greeted with hysterical headlines about the death of English cricket, a story that can be found in more detail later on in this book. At this point, however, no one had actually specified how long a game could last, so some touring matches could go on a little too long. One game in South Africa in 1939 had been played for 12 days before someone on the England team remembered that they were due back in London, so the game had to be drawn to prevent them from missing their boat.

In 1900, the six-ball over was introduced to replace its four- and five-ball predecessors and it has survived to the present day. Australia and New Zealand did experiment with the eight-ball over until as late as 1979, but it was widely agreed that they were making things unnecessarily complicated and they eventually gave it up as a bad idea.

The International Cricket Council (ICC) was formed in 1909 by the MCC and representatives from Australia and South Africa to oversee the global game. Membership was initially limited to members of the British Commonwealth, like India, New Zealand and the West Indies, hence the exclusion of the USA who had been taking it fairly seriously up until that point. It's a reasonable assumption that, had the Americans been allowed to continue, they'd have invented Twenty20 cricket at some point in the 1930s, called it 'SuperStumps' and Sir Don Bradman would have been made to wear gold spandex pants and do adverts for hot dogs.

In 1960, the English began to experiment with a revolutionary new form of cricket, limiting both teams to one innings each, both of which were to be played on the same day. One-day cricket was very popular with supporters, particularly those whose bosses would laugh openly if they ever asked for five days off to watch a Test match. By 1975, this shortened form of the game was so popular that a World Cup was developed which, typically, England have never won.

By 1993, the foreign powers had grown weary with having their global game run by a private members' club in London. The ICC gained autonomy for themselves, eventually moving out of London to swanky new offices in Dubai, where they didn't have to worry so much about corporate tax. The MCC retained the copyright to the rules of cricket and they remain the only people who can change them, it's just that they are expected to run it past the ICC first.

More epoch-shaking than that was the day in 2002 when 11 of the 18 English counties voted in favour of giving a much-reduced version of the game a chance. Stuart Robinson, marketing manager for the England and Wales Cricket Board (ECB), had an idea for a version that could be played in under three hours, without anyone getting bored or having to go to work just when it was getting interesting. Twenty20 cricket was born and it immediately took its place in the mainstream.

Which is pretty much when you came along. Good timing, well done you. More and more people are falling for cricket, seduced by the Twenty20 and then staying for the Test matches. Perhaps you're going to be one of them? Let's find out.

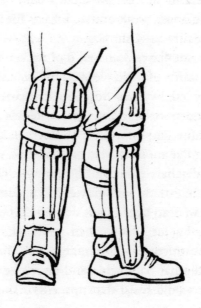

The basics

The game

There's no getting away from the fact that cricket looks pretty complicated. There's a lot of numbers, a lot of silly names and when a commentator says, '5 off the over, 136 for four with 12 still to play,' it can be enough to make even the most determined beginner break down in tears. The funny thing is that it's all actually quite simple.

Now, we've all played some kind of cricket at one stage or another as children, haven't we? Usually on a gloomy British campsite with one of those little sets that comes in a green, shrink-wrapped polythene case and contains one bat, one ball, three stumps and some bails. If your holiday experiences were anything like mine, the bat would be so small that you suspected it may have been built for kittens. The ball would be heavier than lead, the stumps wouldn't go into the ground and the bails were so lightweight that they'd be blown into a farmer's field by the first gust of wind. Nevertheless, the game's central structure would be the same. Your little sister would hold the bat backwards and knock her stumps over first ball. You would insist that this meant she was out and you would be told off by your mum for taking it all too seriously. You would then take the bat and, on your first ball, would accidentally hit it straight up in the air where it would be caught cleanly by your mother who would then make some kind of remark about karma, a remark which you would be unable to hear through your hot, salty tears of frustration. Then your dad would step up and spend 45 minutes repeatedly tonking the ball over the shower block, running backwards and forwards when the ball got lost in the bushes and sometimes clocking up as many as 23 runs at a time. When the tantrums eventually subsided, the cricket set would be hastily given to another family and the afternoon would never be spoken of again.

This, I'm told, is the first memory that most people have of cricket, so it's not really a surprise that so many potential fans are traumatised to the extent that they can't stand to watch it at a professional level.

Anyway, the fact is that you already know the basics. You know that the general idea is to score runs, which you do by running from one marker to another. You know that there are stumps involved that you must protect, you know that if you hit the ball straight up in the air and it is caught, your contribution will be over and you even know that if you hit the ball and it is returned to the marker before you manage to run there, you will be run out. You actually know all the important stuff already, you just don't know how 'proper cricket' works.

The main difference between the campsite game and its professional equivalent is that proper cricket is contested by two teams of eleven players and not by a family of four with some playing to impress, some not entirely sure what they're playing and others who are just glad that they're not on a day-trip to a donkey sanctuary. In the professional game two umpires are in place to keep the peace and you definitely can't run 23 times from one ball. Instead of one set of stumps, there are two and they are placed at either end of a 22-yard strip of very, very short grass known as 'the pitch'.

The batsmen work in pairs to score runs, with one of them at one set of stumps batting and his partner at the opposite end, waiting to run. If the ball is hit well, they both run, passing by each other in the middle and crossing the line just in front of the stumps known as 'the crease' to score a single 'run'. Having now swapped places, their roles are reversed for the next ball. There is a large boundary which surrounds the playing area and if the ball crosses it then four runs are awarded. If the ball crosses it without touching the ground, and it will have to be an almighty big hit to do that, six runs are awarded.

If one of the batsmen is dismissed, for example by hitting the ball up in the air and having it caught, he has to walk off the pitch and is replaced by one of his teammates. Once a batsman is dismissed, or 'out' as it is known, he cannot return. A batsman cannot bat alone so, with an eleven-man team, if ten of them are dismissed, that is the end of that team's turn, or 'innings' as we like to call it. At this point, the other team have their innings, sending two batsmen to the pitch and replacing them one by one when they are out until ten of their eleven men have been dismissed. At this point, their innings being over and their side being 'all out', the two teams compare the amount of runs they have scored and the side with the most wins! How easy was that?

We'll go into the various forms of the game in far more detail as the book progresses, but I just wanted to show you that real cricket is not that far removed from whatever you have played on holiday or at school or with friends down the park, some cans of knock-off cider, a tennis ball and a short plank of wood. It's just a case of scoring more runs than the other team without doing any of the silly things that will result in your being 'out'. We'll have a closer look at those silly things in a moment, but first let's explore the playing area.

The playing area

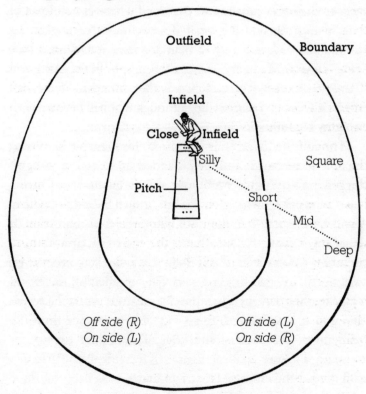

Fig. 1 The areas of a cricket pitch

As you can see from the diagram, cricket is played on a large, roundish field with that small strip of pitch roughly in the middle of it. Sizes differ from one ground to the next, but generally you'll find that all fields are roughly 450–500 feet (135–150m) in diameter.

Much of the confusion in cricket is generated by the strange-sounding names given to the fielders. In cricket, the captain of the fielding team can tell his men to stand anywhere he likes. As long as he has one man bowling and one man as wicket-keeper, the other nine can be deployed wherever he thinks the ball is most likely to be hit. Tell a beginner that England are playing three slips, a gully, a man at covers, a mid-on, a long-off, a short leg, a fine leg and you'll be met with the blankest of blank looks. The names, as odd as they are, denote where the fielders have been placed and, although it will take you a while to learn all of them, some are actually quite simple.

The simplest of all is the wicket-keeper, who I'm sure you'll be able to recognise instantly. Padded up and possessing the biggest pair of gloves you'll ever see, he has to stand behind the stumps and try to catch the little edged balls that come off the bat, or more often than not, just to stop the balls that the batsman misses. Next to him, you can sometimes find a number of other fielders, like spare wicket-keepers, but without all the padding. These chaps are called 'slips'. The one nearest to the 'keeper is the first slip, the next one is the second slip and so on. Usually, there will only be one of these, but sometimes you can see four or five of them lined up.

Have a closer look at figure 1. Imagine the batsman is standing at the stumps. He's right-handed, as the majority of batsmen are. If you split him down the middle, metaphorically at least, everything on the bat side is known as 'the off side', as

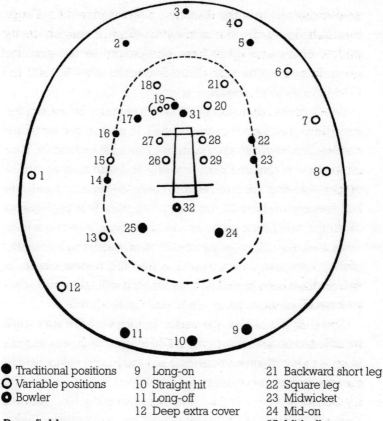

● Traditional positions
○ Variable positions
◉ Bowler

Deep fielders
1   Deep cover point
2   Third man
3   Long stop
4   Deep fine leg
5   Fine leg
6   Deep backward
    square
7   Deep square leg
8   Deep midwicket

9   Long-on
10 Straight hit
11 Long-off
12 Deep extra cover

Short fielders
13 Extra cover
14 Cover
15 Cover point
16 Point
17 Gully
18 Fly slip
19 Slips
20 Leg slip

21 Backward short leg
22 Square leg
23 Midwicket
24 Mid-on
25 Mid-off

Silly
26 Silly mid-off
27 Silly point
28 Short leg
29 Silly mid-on

31 Wicket-keeper
32 Bowler

**Fig. 2 A pitch showing the field
for a right-handed batsman**

if when he hits the ball there he's trying to swat it off him. Everything on his leg side is known as 'the on side' or 'the leg side'. Therefore, if you ever hear the word on, off or leg, you at least know what side of the pitch the fielder is on.

Now it gets even easier. If you hear the word 'long' or 'deep', it means that the fielder is a long way away from the stumps. If you hear the word 'mid', it means they're in the middle. 'Short' means they're quite close and, brilliantly, 'silly' means that you have to be very silly to get that close. So, by that rationale, a mid-on is on the side of the batsman's legs and roughly midway to the boundary, while a long-off must be on the side of the batsman's bat and, well, a long way off.

In a similar vein, anything on a 90-degree angle to the batsman is 'square', while anything behind him would be 'fine'. Therefore, a square leg is off to the side of the batsman on his leg side and a fine leg is on the same side but behind him.

Some of the others, like gully and cover, have their own special names that have evolved over time, but you needn't worry too much about that for now. Familiarity will come in time and we're only just getting started.

What's it all about?

Ok, so you know what the pitch looks like, where the batsman stands and roughly what everyone is trying to achieve. The batsmen are trying to score runs and the bowlers are trying to stop them, preferably by dismissing them and sending them back to the pavilion, the big white building where batsmen go to sulk. The two sides continue to do this until there's no one left to bat, but let's go back to the start.

Every cricket match begins with the toss of a coin. The two team captains and the umpire will gather on the pitch and the official will toss the coin high into the air. The captain who wins the toss will win the right to decide who bats first, his team or his opponent's. Generally, it's a good idea to bat first as it gives your team the initiative and sets the target for the other side, putting them under pressure immediately. However, it might be that the captain will actually enjoy the pressure and will want to know exactly how many runs he needs to win. It all depends on a number of conditions that we're not going to go into just yet but which include the weather and the state of the pitch. Now, you look like the clever type, so let's say that you're the captain and, as you look the lucky type as well, let's say that you've won the toss too. Hurrah! Well done you. What's that now? You're batting? Good stuff. You need to score as many runs as you can while you bat, and then bowl the other team out for less than you scored.

You jog back into the pavilion, tell your two best batsmen to get all their protective equipment on, or to 'pad up' as we call it in the trade, and then you send them out onto the pitch. There, waiting for them with an evil glint in their eyes, is the fielding team. The fielding team's captain selects a bowler and he takes an appropriate run-up, charges in and hurls the ball down the pitch to your batsman. It is down to the batsman to decide what to do. Does he leave the ball or does he try to hit it? If he tries to hit it, he can score runs, but he might also hit it into the air where he can be caught out. Runs are scored by hitting the ball and running from the line in front of your stumps, to the line in front of the other stumps. When both batsman, crossing over in the middle, touch their bats on the ground beyond their line, a run is scored. If they get really good and start hitting the ball over the ropes on the outskirts of the field, they'll score boundaries. Remember, if the ball crosses the rope after bouncing then it's a four. If it crosses the rope without bouncing it's a six.

Limited overs game

The game that we're playing here is a limited overs game. Bowlers bowl in spells of six consecutive balls, or deliveries, as they can be known, at a time. Each six-ball session is known as an 'over'. When the over is complete, they have to give the ball to someone else. Most captains tend to have two bowlers alternating for six or seven overs each before considering a change of tactics. Bowlers aim to dismiss batsmen, or get them out – known as taking wickets – while preventing them from scoring runs. If they can prevent them from scoring a single run in their over, it is known as a 'maiden over' because it is a pure and unsullied over. Seriously.

The limited overs game is a straight, balanced competition between two sides. In this instance let's say that it's a 50-over game. Both teams receive 50 overs (300 deliveries with six deliveries per over) and from these they must score as many runs as possible. Then the other team will have their turn, with the same amount of overs, and will attempt to score more. If they do, they win.

There are a lot of numbers on display in cricket, which is one of the principal reasons that people get confused. The main number is the team's score. This is the total number of runs scored by all of the batsmen put together. If, after 20 overs, your first man has scored 50 runs and his partner has scored 50 runs, then the team will have 100 runs altogether. This will be expressed as '100 without loss', or 100-0. This is because, so far, your team haven't lost any wickets, a success that I put down entirely to your calm guidance from the pavilion. Now, in the next over, your first batsman takes an almighty swing and there's a loud crack as the ball blasts the stumps clean out of the ground. He's out, he's heading back to the pavilion and, if I were you, I'd avoid him for a bit, he's liable to be a bit grumpy. Your team has lost a wicket. They are now 100 for one, or 100-1. The next man goes in and he scores a four before the end of the over. Now, after 21 overs, your team are on 104-1. 104 is the total amount of runs (50+50+4) and the 1 is the poor opening batsman who was dismissed.

Let's go back to the running. When the batsman hits a ball and runs down the other end, he ends up in the reverse position to his partner. The man facing the balls is known as the 'striker' and is at 'the striker's end'. The other batsman, not facing a ball, stands at the 'non-striker's end', picking his nose and waiting to run. He can't get too comfortable though. At the end of every over, the batsmen have to swap places. Some batsmen, greedy for strike, will deliberately score an odd number of runs on the final ball of the over so that they end up at the non-striker's end and then get to go back to the striker's end for the first ball of the next over.

Right, back to the game. It's the 22nd over and your second batsman, the one on 50, is at the striker's end. He scores a single, which sends him to the non-striker's end and the new bloke is back up on strike. He scored a four, so he must be good, eh? Ah … apparently not. He's out. He goes to block the ball, it gets the slightest of edges from the bat and the wicket-keeper behind the stumps catches him out. The score is now 105-2.

Getting the hang of it? Of course you are. The second number is of vital importance because it gives you a read on how healthy the team's chances are of surviving much longer. You know that there are eleven players in your team? Well, you can't bat on your own, so when that number reaches ten, it's all over. Interestingly though, cricket scores are never expressed as, say, 105-10. At this point, you see, it is obvious that the team is done, so the score becomes 105 all out. It has a ring of finality about it, doesn't it?

Back to the game, anyway. You are the fourth batsman in and you go out and score 25 runs, while your partner, the second man in, has now picked up 75 runs. So, with the first batsman's 50 and the third chap's 4, that makes 154. Not bad at all. In fact, it gets even better. You get 50, your partner gets 100 and you end up on 204-2 at the end of the 50 overs. Now it's time for the other team to have a go.

You nip back to the pavilion, have some lunch and then, approximately 45 minutes later, you're ready to start. This time, you're the fielding team, so you pick a bowler and wait to get stuck in. Now remember, your team scored 204 runs. That's the target for the other team to beat. There are, therefore, two ways for you to win. The first is for you to bowl them out, which is a catch-all term for taking their wickets whichever way you can, before they reach your batting score. The second is simply to slow them down so much that their 50 overs elapse before they can reach the target. What tends to happen is that the fielding team start off by trying to frustrate their opponents and then reap the benefits of anxious batsmen who suddenly start trying to hit everything as hard as they can in an effort to meet their target. Anxious batsmen make mistakes.

Your team do this and they do it well, almost certainly because of your excellent leadership. You chop and change your bowlers to keep them fresh, and they take the wickets. After ten overs, the score is 30-3. You've taken three wickets and they've only scored 30 runs in what amounts to 20 per cent of their allotted overs. At 20 overs, you have them 70-7. They're on the run! They've only got three wickets left and they still need 135 to win! They get back into the game after 30 overs, refusing to lose any more wickets and lifting the score to 100-7 but they've now only got 20 overs left. Do they hit out and try to get the 105 runs they need? They do and it costs them dearly. You bowl them all out for just 124 runs. They are 81 runs short of the target with no one left to bat. You win!

Test match cricket

The other style of the game is 'first-class cricket' or 'Test match cricket'. This is a much more sophisticated game with no restriction on the amount of overs in an innings, but an extended time limit of four or five days. Teams now have two chances to bat, still aiming to score more runs than each other. However, they can only win the match if their opponents have completed both of their innings, otherwise it's a draw.

Let's say that you're batting first. It's a five-day game and you can spend as much time as you like out there, scoring runs as slowly and carefully as you see fit. You take two days to score 500 all out. On the third day, your opponents get their turn and they score 301 all out. You now have a second chance to bat, but there are only two days left. You have a lead of 199, but you can only win the match if your opponents have completed both of their innings and at the moment, they've only completed one. This means that you have to make a choice. How much of the remaining time do you want to spend batting and how much bowling? The more time you spend scoring runs, the higher your lead and the less chance of the opposition being able to chase it. Unfortunately, it also lessens the chance of you being able to bowl them all out.

So, you go out to bat on day four and you score 150-4 by the lunch break. You now lead by 349. You look at the fact that they scored 301 the last time and you decide that they are unlikely to do much better than that. You gamble, essentially, on them failing to score 350 runs. However, in order to make them bat, your innings has to finish. Thankfully, this doesn't mean ordering your batsman to put their bats on their heads and commit cricket-suicide; there's a far simpler way. You just 'declare' and end the innings there and then. With lunch and both of your innings complete, there is a day and a half left to play with. If the opposition score 350, they will win the game. If they are bowled out, you win. If neither of those scenarios occurs by the end of the fifth day, say for example that they score 250-6, then it is a draw.

Test match cricket, therefore, is not simply a battle of run-scoring, it's far more complicated than that. It is a battle of strategy. How quickly do you bat? How well can you balance a need to score runs with a need to take wickets? How confident are you in the ability of your bowlers?

Sometimes things go wrong. Horribly, horribly wrong. If the first team to bat sets a really high score and the second team don't come anywhere near it, there can be hideous consequences, known as a 'follow on'. If the second team to bat fall 200 runs or more short of their predecessors, the opposing captain can force them to bat again. This is not only a public humiliation, but it's also a very strong sign that you're going to lose. Having just been bowled out once, the chances are that it will happen again and, with anything less than 200, you'll lose the game by an innings. The other team won't even need to pad up for their second innings. How embarrassing.

The one thing you can't control is the weather and that can often play a part, especially if the game is being played in the UK. If it rains, all the cricketers run inside and the game cannot continue. Even if you only have to take one more wicket to win the game, when the first raindrops start to splatter in the outfield, you still have to go off. The weather can be very frustrating, especially if you've got a specific plan in mind. That, though, is all part of the game.

The team

There are eleven men in a cricket team, one of whom will be the captain and another who will be the wicket-keeper. From the eleven, at least four will be chosen purely for their ability to bowl the ball and take the wickets of the opposing batsmen. The rest will be selected for their ability to score runs.

Generally speaking, a cricket captain tends to send his batsmen out in order of quality. The opening batsmen (1, 2) will be the men that he believes can put down the foundation of a good innings. They will need to be able to face up to the opposition's best bowlers, who will be at their freshest and most dangerous. An opening batsman should always be looking to score at least 50 runs, which is known as a 'half-century'. However, 100 runs is the real target. Every batsman wants to grab a century.

The third man in (3) will need to be a man for all seasons. If one of the opening batsmen (openers) loses his wicket quickly, number 3 will have to go in and stay calm, making sure that the team don't lose another man in quick succession. Too many wickets in a short space of time can precipitate a panicky collapse and a disastrous innings. However, that won't always be the case. Sometimes he'll be following an excellent innings and he may be charged with going out and hitting some quick runs. A versatile cricketer is always a good number 3.

The middle-order batsmen (4, 5 and 6) will be expected to get themselves settled quickly because, unless the opening batsmen have really had a bad day, they won't always have a lot of time to play with. This is especially the case in limited overs cricket, where they may join the game towards the closing stages. They would tend to score between 25 and 50 runs, although you wouldn't be surprised if one of them scored a century.

Wicket-keepers will be chosen for their catching skills, but they all know that they must be able to bat as well. A standard position for a 'keeper is the top end of the bottom half (7), although there have been a number of them over the years who have batted higher up the order, some even going so far as to open for their teams.

The rest of the batsmen will almost certainly have been picked primarily as bowlers. They are known as 'the tail-end' (8, 9, 10 and 11) and very little is expected of them, especially the last man in. A good team will have bowlers who can bat, but that is still rather rare. If your average tail-ender scores 50 runs the usual reaction is one of surprise, or horror if you're the captain of the fielding team.

Some teams, although not so many at international level these days, have a number 11 who is as good at batting as you or I. They are known as 'bunnies', because they stand in front of the bowler looking as terrified as rabbits in front of the headlights of an oncoming juggernaut. Any runs from a bunny are considered a fortunate blip.

Ways of 'getting out'

There are ten different ways that a batsman can be dismissed, so pay attention. Imagine that you're a batsman about to go in for your team. You want to score runs and help to win the game, but you won't be much good if you're out too quickly. All dismissals are signalled with the raised index finger of the umpire, the worst sight in cricket. Here's what you have to do to avoid it.

Fig. 3 The umpire signalling 'out'

1. Bowled

This one is very simple. You know those stumps that you're standing in front of? Don't let the ball hit them, whatever you do. Swing the bat, hit the ball. Don't miss, because it's a horrible noise. Anyone who has ever wielded a bat could tell you the feeling you get when you hear that fateful clunk. You don't even need to turn around to know what has happened. It's not just the stumps, though. If either one of those two bails, the little bits of wood atop the stumps, are dislodged, then you've been bowled and it's time to make way for the next man.

2. Caught

As soon as you hit the ball into the air, you're in danger of being out. It's tempting to hit the ball high so that it travels a long distance, but it's a dangerous tactic. It's far safer to keep it on the ground because you can't be caught that way. Remember, if the ball hits your bat, or even your hand, and is caught by a fielder before it has touched the ground, then that's your lot, you're out.

3. Lbw

Now, this is a tricky one, so we're going to have a closer look at this later. Essentially, the rule is in place to stop people trying to put a part of their body, usually their legs, in-between the ball and the stumps. If the umpire believes that the ball would have hit the stumps had it not been for you sticking a leg in the way, he'll dismiss you.

4. Run out

Now have a look at that diagram of the cricket pitch (page 21). Do you see those two lines that run just in front of the stumps? They are the creases. The one nearest the bowler is the one you have to run to if you want to do your bit to score a run; the one nearest you is the one that your partner must cross. If the ball is returned to either set of stumps before the nearest player reaches his designated crease, putting at least a part of his bat down on the ground behind the line, that player is 'run out'.

5. Stumped

Back to creases for this one. The one by your feet is the limit of your safe territory. If you step out of here to hit the ball and you miss it, the wicket-keeper can catch the ball and hit the stumps with it to 'stump' you. If you want to be safe, you need to stay behind this line...

6. Hit wicket

...Not too far behind the line, though. If you're too close to the stumps, there's a chance that you could knock them over yourself and, as I tried to convince my little sister in the introduction, that's enough to see you out. Those bails have to stay on and it doesn't matter if it's you or anyone else who knocks them over. Don't worry about them being blown off by the wind, though: that's absolutely fine.

7. Hit the ball twice

Now, this is an interesting one. Imagine that you clip a ball with the bottom of your bat and it sneaks off towards your stumps. You jab your bat at it and flick it away just before it knocks the bails off. Are you out? Actually, no. You are allowed to hit the ball twice to protect your stumps, but anything else and you're out. Before this rule was introduced there was nothing to stop a batsman repeatedly hitting the ball as many times as it took to get it away, an inglorious practice that led to a number of fatalities as they accidentally bludgeoned any fielder daft enough to get in their way.

8. Obstructing the field

Obstruction works in two ways. The most obvious example is to physically prevent the fielders from carrying out their duties, by, for example, trying to avoid a run-out by blocking the ball with your bat or body. But obstruction can be by word as well as deed. If a batsman hits a shot high into the air, he has to take his chances. He cannot, as the ball falls to earth, shout out, 'Oh my God, it's Elvis!' in the hope that the fielder will look behind him and miss the catch. That's obstruction as well.

9. Handled the ball

If the batsman's hand is on the bat, it is counted as the bat, hence the fact that you can be out when the ball hits your glove and is caught by the wicket-keeper. However, if the hand isn't on the bat then it shouldn't be anywhere near the ball. Former England captain Graham Gooch was once given out when he slapped away a ball that had the temerity to bounce languidly off his bat towards the stumps.

10. Timed out

Quite a rare one, this, but it remains in place to prevent time-wasting. If a batsman takes more than three minutes to get out on to the pitch to replace his dismissed colleague then he can be timed out. This has never happened in test cricket, but it has happened occasionally at the lower levels, usually because of freakish circumstances or injuries. One poor batsman, crippled with a groin strain, took three minutes to limp out on to the pitch only to have the fielders appeal successfully for his dismissal before he got there. Then he had to limp back.

11. Retired

Alright, so this is number 11, but really it belongs in a category of its own. A batsman can end his innings through injury (retired hurt), if he can no longer continue, or through choice (retired out), if he doesn't want to. Two high-scoring Sri Lankan batsmen went for the latter in a 2001 match against Bangladesh in order to give their teammates a go.

Leg before wicket (lbw)

Ok, brace yourself, we're going into the lbw zone. Like the offside rule in football, lbw is one of the most contentious, controversial and misunderstood rules in the game, which is a shame really because it should all be so simple. After all, the clue is in the name: leg before wicket.

Introduced to stop nefarious individuals sticking their legs in front of the stumps and blocking the ball, lbw has a number of clauses which continue to confuse fans of all ages. You might be tentatively approaching cricket, assuming yourself to know very little, but I can assure you that a great number of regular observers still can't get their heads round this rule. So let's have a look at it, shall we?

All lbw decisions, for all of the faffing around beforehand, must eventually come down to one crucial question: was the ball going to hit the stumps? It's not an easy question to answer. Even with television replays, experts can still find it difficult to accurately predict the movement of the ball. The introduction of Hawkeye technology, a kind of hi-tech tracking system, has made it easier for the pundits, but the umpires don't get the benefit of that knowledge. They have to stand out on the field, surrounded by excited players, trying to make the decision on the basis of what they've seen with their own eyes.

Incidentally, one of the stranger aspects of cricket is that the umpire cannot give a man out for lbw unless someone on the fielding team appeals. The traditional way to appeal is to ask the umpire, 'How was that?' Over the centuries this has blurred into the English 'Howzat?', the Australian, 'Owwazaaaaat?' and the Sri Lankan 'AHHHHHWAZZAAAAAAAAAT?' For some reason, the Sri Lankan team always seem to be under the impression that the umpire is outside the stadium and unable to hear them.

Anyway, back to the basics. If the ball was going to hit the stumps and it hits the batsman's body, usually his leg unless he's standing in a very strange position, he is out lbw. Unless…

1 …the ball pitches down the leg side and then cuts in and hits the batsman. Then it's not out because you can't be given out with a leg-side ball.
2 …the ball pitches down the off side and then cuts in and hits the batsman outside of the line of the stumps while he is attempting to play a shot. Only if you're standing there with a blank look on your face and the bat poised can you be given out in this way. Playing a shot gets you out of trouble.
3 …the ball hits the bat or the glove and then hits the pads. This is colloquially known as 'bat-pad' and is not an offence.

The batsman should always be given out if…

1 …the ball pitches on that strip you can see in p. 37, the one that runs from wicket to wicket, and hits the batsman while still on the same line. We call this a 'plumb' decision.

2 ...the ball pitches outside off stump and then hits the batsman in line with the strip.

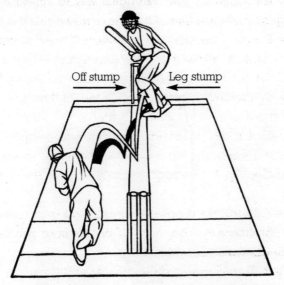

Off stump ⟶   ⟵ Leg stump

Fig. 4 Ways in which you can be bowled out leg before wicket

The umpire is unlikely to give an lbw if the batsman has come forwards out of his crease. It's very difficult to tell how a ball will react over a short distance and practically impossible over more than a few yards. Was it going to go over the stumps, was it going to gently veer away? If the umpire can't tell, he won't give it.

Lbw decisions should never be disputed by the player. Indeed, it is considered poor form to give any indication of your displeasure with the umpire. Standing your ground and glaring at him is definitely out. Even stomping off the pitch, shaking your head in disbelief, is going too far. In fact, players are expected to help the umpire make his decision. It may be an archaic Corinthian ideal, but there are still players who will walk straight off without waiting to see that raised finger.

4

The techniques

Batting basics

So if there are that many ways to get out, how on earth do you stay in? Well, batting is essentially a balancing act between aggression and caution. The more eager the batsman is to slap and swing at the ball, the more runs he will score, but the more likely it is that he will be heading back to the pavilion with his head hung low before too long. Not every ball has to be hit hard. Sometimes it's better just to block it and bide your time while you grow accustomed to the speed of the ball and the bounce of the pitch. Mind you, the more defensive a batsman is, the fewer runs he will score. It's a tricky one, isn't it?

Ultimately, the batsman's tactics will depend upon his circumstances and this is one of the many reasons that cricket is one of the finest sports on the planet. Every game pans out differently. Very few players are ever granted the luxury of picking and choosing how to make the most of their innings. Opening batsmen, the first men on the pitch when the innings begins, may have a few overs or even a whole session to call their own, but it won't last long. Sooner or later, they will find themselves under pressure either to stay in, or to hit out and get some runs.

Different players have different strengths. Some like to wait for balls that travel down the side of their leg so that they can whip them to the boundaries. Others like the balls that stay on the side of their bat, their off side, so that they can drive them away. Some balls will hit the ground quickly and rear up to waist height or even higher, and there are players who sit and wait for these ones and then hook them high into the air for six. Others relish the ones that pop up off the pitch late, the lower balls. But whatever style of ball they are comfortable with, as soon as the bowler realises their preferences, they'll be lucky to see another one all innings.

The best batsmen have a range of shots at their disposal and the intelligence and temperament to know when to use them. It is imperative that a batsman concentrates for every ball because the bowler will always be looking for the advantage. No batsman wants to be dismissed without scoring any runs. This is known as a 'duck' and it is the most shameful and humiliating thing that can happen to a batsman. I should know, I've had a few of them. In fact, when I used to disgrace myself for my school team on a regular basis, I even managed the rare feat of a 'golden duck'. This is when a batsman is so hapless that he walks out to the stumps and is dismissed on his first ball.

Varieties of batting

There are a variety of shots that any batsman can use in a match and they depend on two major factors: first, their ability to judge the destination of the ball and, second, their proficiency with the shot style. Some batsmen excel at one type of shot, but struggle with others. Sometimes it's best to just not bother with a ball rather than amateurishly swing at it. Nevertheless, here's a quick guide to the most common strokes.

Leave it

This is often the wisest choice that any batsman can make, assuming that the ball isn't heading directly at the stumps. Leaving one of those would be a bad idea. Anything passing wide of the off stump is a tease, the bowler trying to make you hang the bat out and clip it to the slips. Anything going down the leg side could be given as a wide. Decisions obviously depend on the state of the game. A batsman attempting to stem a flow of wickets in a Test match would be quite happy to leave a succession of balls just to wear out the bowler and get used to the pitch. A batsman doing the same in a Twenty20 game risks the wrath of his teammates if he lets anything go by without at least trying to hit it.

Block it

If the ball is zeroing in on your stumps, then you've really got to do something about it. A good straight bat along the line of delivery is all that is required to gently tap back to the bowler. The bat must be angled slightly down towards the pitch to prevent it popping back up for the bowler to catch, but as long as it is kept straight and in a vertical line, it should always stop the ball. Bowlers can get very frustrated by defensive blocks. Imagine walking all the way back to the run-up point, pounding in on the stumps, hurling the ball as fast as you can at the batsman and all he does is block it. Again and again and again. Even though he wasn't scoring any runs, you'd lose your sense of humour very quickly. You'd bowl something outside of off stump and 'thwock', off it would zip to the boundary.

Drive it

If the ball pitches near the batsman's feet and starts to rise up to anywhere underneath knee-cap level, then it is fit for driving. There are three major categories of drive. The straight drive is fairly self-explanatory, but is actually one of the most difficult shots to play. It is far more natural to drive it across your body or even away from your body in the opposite direction. If you choose to hit it away from your body, which for a right-handed batsman would be a shot towards his right side, then it is an off drive. If it is driven the other way, it is an on drive. These shots, when executed well, are some of the most elegant in the game. It's not so much about the power of the swing, but more about the timing. If the ball hits the middle of the bat at the right time, it will zip off like an Exocet.

Sweep it

By and large, most fielders will be standing in front of you, so why not try to score by hitting it behind you? Because it's very difficult, is the simple answer. The batsman must be absolutely sure of where the ball will pitch and how it will behave, but if he gets it right, it can be a valuable source of runs. Anything down the leg side and pitched near the batsman is sweepable. We call it a sweep because of the action of pulling the bat horizontally across the body just above ground level, as if you're trying to use it to sweep dust and cobwebs off the pitch. Sometimes the batsman will drop to one knee to get a better action. Timed well, the ball will shoot off in-between the wicket-keeper and the square-leg fielder into a nice big gap. That said, a fine-leg or a backward-short-leg fielder would render this shot worthless.

Cut it

If the ball is delivered down the off side and then rears up high, the batsman should be looking to cut it away from him. This is another shot for a horizontal bat and it's one that requires absolutely perfect timing. The face of the bat must be angled either straight or pointing slightly towards the ground to ensure that the ball doesn't fly through the air at a catchable level. Some batsmen, the really brave ones, like the altitude and will open the face of the bat to ensure that it does go up. This can work on a close field, as the ball will go over the fielders' heads, or in Twenty20, when you're actively trying to hit sixes. However, it's not a particularly wise tactic in Test cricket, where wickets are at a premium.

Pull it

Anything that bounces up at waist height is just asking to be pulled away. This involves the batsman pulling the bat around the body from the off side towards the leg side, rather like a sweep, but at greater altitude. Ideally, as with the cut, the bat should be angled towards the ground to prevent it flying up in the air. The timing of the impact determines the destination of the ball. A late contact will send it further backwards towards fine leg, an earlier one towards square leg. Depending on the fielding positions, this can be the difference between an unfortunate dismissal and another boundary.

Hook it

Bowlers may think that a bouncer can disable or disorientate any batsman, but there is one weapon that he may have in his arsenal. The hook shot is one of the most exciting in the game, but it's very, very difficult to get right. The batsman has to raise a horizontal bat almost to helmet level to make contact with the ball. The increased height of the shot makes mistakes much more likely. Hook a bouncer and you're either going to spank it for six or power it up like a rocket, leaving you to stand in horror and watch it descend to the grateful hands of the fielder.

Paddle-scoop it

Erm … yeah. This odd little shot is so new that we're still not entirely sure what to call it. Paddle-scoop will do for now, but you may hear it referred to as a 'frying-pan' or 'head-flick', or even a 'Dilshan' or 'Dilscoop' after the Sri Lankan player who seems to have invented it. Essentially, the bat is held out in front of the batsman like a frying pan and then, when the ball arrives, the bat is lifted up in the air and over the head, flicking the ball up and over the wicket-keeper and behind to an area where no one ever puts a fielder. It is one of the most difficult shots in cricket and one of the most dangerous. Get the timing even slightly wrong and you're more likely to crash the ball into your face than to score any runs.

Switch hit it

Switch hitting is the most extraordinary development in batting for hundreds of years and it's not something that you can learn easily. As we've already discussed, fielders are deployed specifically to prevent batsmen playing their favourite shots. They change dramatically when a left-handed batsman comes in because the range of shots he plays is reversed. But what can you do when a batsman stands in a right-handed position and then, as the ball is bowled, alters his stance, shifts the bat in his hand and suddenly becomes left-handed? Whole swathes of the pitch are unoccupied and he can aim at them with impunity. Mind you, first he has to be one of those rare human beings capable of playing with either hand. It was Kevin Pietersen who first popularised this shot while playing for England and it was so controversial that the MCC, the owners of the rules of cricket, had to be consulted to make sure it was actually a legal shot. To their eternal credit, they decided that switch hitting was exciting, innovative and good for the game as a whole. Who says they're out of touch at the MCC?

Bowling basics

Bowling is about so much more than just trying to hit the stumps. Perhaps it's a good tactic for a game in the park but, with the exception of the bunnies, it doesn't work so well in the professional game. Even the worst batsmen can usually block up their stumps for a while. The trick is to make them do something very silly.

Imagine that you're opening the batting for your team in a Test match. You've got five days ahead of you and there's nothing but glorious sunshine in the forecast, so you're in no hurry at all. If anything comes down your leg side, you'll sweep it off along the ground. If anything is delivered with width, which means that it would miss your off stump by some distance, you have a go at hitting that for four. Anything in the middle and you simply block it away. So far, so good. But what about a ball that's a little bit outside of your stumps, but not very much? And it's quite high, but not so high that you can really have a swing at it? Hit or block? If the ball is approaching you at 90mph, which is the speed of a good fast bowler, you won't get very much time to decide. That's why most bowlers tend to try to make the ball bounce in that danger zone, just a little above and a little outside that off stump. It's the position that's hardest to gauge and most likely to result in a little clip to the wicket-keeper or the slips.

Other bowlers may be really crafty and try to frustrate you. Realising that you're only going to block if it comes towards your stumps, they simply repeat the process again and again and again. Sooner or later, you'll be panicking that you haven't scored any runs. And then the bowler will pitch one short, which is to say that it will hit the ground quickly and bounce up nice and high and hittable. 'I'll have some of that,' you'll say and you'll heave away at it with your bat. The trouble is that you weren't planning to do this, you were planning to block and you're a little slow off the mark. You make contact with the ball too late to send it high over the boundary ropes, but just in time to send it high into the air and straight to the man at covers. It's so silly and so frustrating and so upsetting, but almost every single innings of cricket ever played will have had at least one dismissal like this.

Bowlers can approach the batsman from either side of the stumps, allowing them to pick the best angle of attack. If the hand holding the ball is the one nearest to the stumps, it is known as 'over the wicket'. Over the wicket bowling means that the angle between the ball and the batsman is minimised. If the hand holding the ball is the one furthest away from the stumps, then it is 'around the wicket' bowling. This allows the bowler to send the ball across the batsman at something of an angle, enabling him to tease his quarry with balls that only need the tiniest of nicks to find the slip fielders.

The really nasty bowlers have one extra weapon in their locker: the bouncer. If a ball is pitched short, impacting the ground halfway down the pitch instead of all the way up near the batsman, it will bounce high into the air. Its height and power will be affected by the speed of the delivery and the size of the bowler. In other words, if a 6ft 4in fast bowler slams a delivery down the pitch at 90mph, duck. Bouncers not only unsettle batsmen, but the few who are brave enough to take a swing at it will usually succeed only in edging it up into the air.

Some bowlers don't bother with speed at all; they try to spin the ball at the batsman to confuse him. This puts the batsman in a rather awkward position. Does he run off his crease to try to intercept the ball before it hits the ground and goes haywire, or will that only make a stumping more likely? Does he stay back and wait to see what happens? Will he even have time to react? Spin bowlers, when they get the movement they want, are a nightmare.

Varieties of bowling

Bowlers, as we've discussed, come in a variety of forms. They range in pace, style and standard and there's one for every occasion. Fast bowlers (seamers and swingers) tend to rely on pace and positioning, while spinners (leg and off) use their wrists or their fingers to send the ball spiralling towards a new and unexpected target. It's important to have a good knowledge of what the different bowlers can do and how they can 'hurt' batsmen, so let's have a closer look at how it all works.

Seamers

The seam of the ball is vital to the way that it behaves when it pitches. A brand new ball will have a prominent seam that juts out away from its body. If a bowler can make it land hard on the seam, it will change its course, either towards the stumps or away towards the wicket-keeper and the waiting slips. Seamers bowl the ball fast, sometimes getting it up to speeds of over 90mph. They can be terrifying to face, especially for the lower order batsmen, but as the ball gets old and the seam gets thumped down and flattened, their powers decrease.

Swingers

Stop giggling at the back. Swingers can make the ball move magically in mid-air as it approaches the batsman, forcing a delivery that seems to be heading for off stump to ease out towards the slips and that's when mistakes happen. It's all to do with aerodynamics affected by the surface of the ball, the rate at which it spins and the level of moisture in the air. A ball with one shiny side and one battered side can move in mysterious ways indeed, especially on an overcast day. Reverse swing is when the ball moves in mid-air, but towards the batsman and his stumps. This kind of movement is very difficult to achieve, but does result in a very, very worried batsman and a large number of successful lbw appeals.

Leg spinners

It can be difficult to remember how spin bowlers are characterised, given the illogical nature of their names. For example, you might think that a leg spinner would be someone who spun the ball around your legs, but that's not actually the case. The leg bit refers to the place the ball pitches; the danger is in where the ball goes after it lands. A leg spinner will land the ball on the leg side and then watch as it veers off towards the off side. Leg spinners can occasionally change their style and bounce the ball from off to leg, an unexpected change of direction which is known as a 'googly'. No-one likes a googly. Just when you've got the hang of one thing...

Off spinners

Off spinners specialise in landing the ball on the off side and spinning it towards the legs or, in many cases, the stumps. A good off spinner will be able to alter the rate of spin on the ball, creating a range of deliveries that deviate violently or even not at all. Sometimes it's actually much worse if the ball doesn't spin, especially if a particularly nasty bowler has delivered the last eleven balls in exactly the same way and then drops a normal one in just when you're least expecting it. Off spinners can occasionally get the ball to land on the leg side and pitch towards the off. This unexpected change of delivery is called a 'doosra' and it's not very pleasant to face at all.

Fielding basics

Fielding may be one of the most boring jobs in cricket, but it's also one of the most important. Every single man out there, whether he's scratching his bottom, picking his nose or absently gazing at aeroplanes passing overhead, has been put in his place for a reason. It could be that the batsman always likes to hit it high in the air down his leg side and the fielder is there to catch him out. It could be that the batsman always likes to hit it high in the air down his leg side and the fielder is there to convince him otherwise, thus slowing down the rate of runs. Not every fielder is in place to make a catch, some are there simply as a diversion.

The captain must make sure that he deploys his fielders to complement his bowlers. A cricket captain has far more influence over his teammates than his counterparts have in any other sport. There are coaches and technical behind-the-scenes teams in cricket, but you won't ever see them standing on the sidelines bellowing out instructions. The captain runs the whole show for himself and fielding is one of the most important disciplines. There's very little point in putting six men on the leg side, if the bowler is going to bowl everything to the off side. Good communication is vital. If a bowler is accurate enough to land a ball in the same place every single time, a captain can set a field that will make it impossible for the batsman to score runs. Until the bowler makes a mistake, of course. Then it all goes wrong.

Generally speaking, the closer the fielders are to the batsman, the more aggressive the field. With lots of men up close, there is more chance of taking advantage of the little nicks and edges that pop up as a batsman tires. A close field also encourages the batsman to take chances by going for the big hits into the unoccupied space. Likewise, a wide and well-spread field will concede lots of singles, but will usually be able to stop the boundaries.

Slip fielders need to have complete concentration to be ready for every single ball that comes their way. They must have superhuman reflexes because, if they do get a chance to make a catch, it's almost certainly going to be coming at them at a fair rate of knots. Slip fielders are not just there to catch either. Working with the wicket-keeper, they can create a poisonous atmosphere for the batsman by whispering snidey comments about his technique, his body odour or even his wife. This is called 'sledging' and there's a whole section at the end of the book devoted to it (see p. 107).

Sometimes you'll see a fielder so close to the batsman that he has to wear a helmet. These chaps are called 'silly mid-offs' or 'silly mid-ons' depending on which side they're standing. There may well be a fine line between bravery and stupidity, but these guys haven't been told about it.

The outfield, the area of the field furthest from the action, is traditionally a depository for bowlers who are waiting to have a turn with the ball. It can be very lonely out there, especially at professional level where the fans will be only too happy to remind a player of his shortfalls. Concentration is key, though. If there's going to be a lofted shot, one of those horrible ones that rise high into the air and come at the fielder out of the sun, this is where it will land.

Fielders need to return the ball back to either the wicket-keeper or the bowler as quickly as possible in order to prevent the batsmen from running. Good fielding is vital in a Test match, essential in a 50-over game and one of the most important components of a Twenty20 match. Bad fielders won't just prevent the team from taking wickets, they'll cost them runs as well and that's not a good combination.

The numbers

Scorecards
The batting card

Scorecards can be very confusing for the beginner, but they're vital if you want to improve your understanding of the game. There's a lot of information in a very small space, but if you know what you're looking at, you'll find that you can glean all the key events of a match with just a glance. Overleaf is one from a made-up Twenty20 match between the made-up villages of Steeple Burpington and Rumpstead-on-Rye.

So, what can we tell from that? Well, you only need to look at the bottom of the scorecard to find out the result. Steeple Burpington won by 95 runs. Their first two batsmen, Grady and Ryan, got them off to a good start by scoring 30 and 63 respectively. Then Rollett came in and scored 42 without being dismissed. The same can't be said for Ratcliffe, who left after hitting 36, to be replaced by McClaren who ended with 7 not out. There were 8 extras, something we'll look at in the next section. Steeple Burpington used all of their 20 overs and with all of their scores added together they ended up with 186 runs after losing just three wickets (Grady, Ryan and Ratcliffe).

Steeple Burpington vs Rumpstead-on-Rye (Steeple Burpington won the toss and elected to bat first)

Steeple Burpington Innings

M Grady	c Fuhrman	b Warren	30
S Ryan		b Gallagher	63
T Rollett*	not out		42
A Ratcliffe	st Rance	b Pearson	36
R McClaren	not out		7
Extras (w 1, nb 1, lb 2, b 4)			8
Total (20 overs)			186-3

Did Not Bat – J Freedman, J Davie+, D Jamieson, R Davies, R Lloyd, R Trumpton

Rumpstead-on-Rye Innings

S Nickless		b Lloyd	23
D Bourke*		lbw Lloyd	4
T Fuhrman	c Davie	b Jamieson	8
J Findlay		lbw Trumpton	0
A Birley	c Davie	b Lloyd	4
D Adams	run out		12
P Rance+		b Davies	7
M Gallagher	c Freedman	b Jamieson	12
T Warren		b Lloyd	4
A Pearson	not out		7
I Macintosh		b Lloyd	0
Extras (w 2, lb 4, b 4)			10
Total (12.1 overs)			91 all out

Steeple Burpington won by 95 runs

How did those wickets go down? Finding out is easy, it's all in the letters that precede or follow the names on the card:

b   identifies the bowler
c   identifies the catcher
lbw   indicates that the dismissal was for leg before wicket
st   indicates a stumping by the wicket-keeper
*   identifies the captain
+   identifies the wicket-keeper

So, with that information in hand, let's see what happened. Grady was caught by Fuhrman, from the bowling of Warren. Ryan was bowled by Gallagher. Ratcliffe was stumped by Rance from the bowling of Pearson. Simple, isn't it? The bowler is always identified, even if the wicket was a catch, because it was his bowling that forced a mistake. He isn't mentioned after a run-out because it's difficult to say that a run-out was caused by good bowling. Not that that stops some bowlers from trying to take the credit.

Let's have a look at the pathetic efforts of Rumpstead-on-Rye, shall we? Things seemed to start quite well for them with a 23 from Nickless, but he was bowled by Lloyd and that seems to have started something of a collapse. Only two other batsmen, Adams and Gallagher, managed to score double figures. Davie took two catches, which is no surprise as you can see that he's the wicket-keeper. Lloyd had a corking game, picking up five wickets and Rumpstead were put to the sword. Not only did they fail to get anywhere near the target, they also failed to even use all of their time. They only lasted for 12 overs and one ball. Appalling stuff.

The bowling card

As well as batting cards like these, there are also bowling cards to enable you to see the other side of the story. Here's the cards from this match.

Rumpstead-on-Rye Bowling	O	M	R	W
Warren	4	0	32	1
Pearson	4	0	34	1
Macintosh	4	0	58	0
Gallagher	4	1	28	1
Birley	4	1	34	0

Steeple Burpington Bowling	O	M	R	W
Lloyd	4	1	26	5
Jamieson	3	0	23	2
Anandanadarajah	2	0	17	1
Davies	2	0	19	1
Freedman	1.1	0	6	0

So, what have we got here? More numbers, more letters, but it's all quite easy to figure out:

O the amount of overs bowled by the bowler
M the amount of maiden overs (overs in which no runs were scored whatsoever)
R the amount of runs scored against the bowler's bowling
W the amount of wickets credited to the bowler

From this we can see that none of the Rumpstead bowlers can be particularly pleased with their efforts. They all had four overs, but none of them could take more than a single wicket. Macintosh and Birley couldn't even manage one. Gallagher can at least claim to have been the most useful, as his wicket only cost the team 28 runs. Warren's and Pearson's were slightly more expensive. Birley was no use whatsoever. He managed to bowl one perfect, maiden over, but before you praise him, remember that those 34 runs would essentially have come from just three overs. Macintosh was actually more of a hindrance than a help. Not only did he fail to take a wicket, but his bowling was apparently so predictable that Steeple Burpington cleaned up, taking 58 runs from it. If he had any shame, he'd drive straight home after the game and bury his head under the duvet.

The Steeple Burpington bowlers had far more to celebrate. First we've got Lloyd who took five wickets for just 26 runs. This is commonly known as a 'five-for', which is always shortened to a 'fifer' and then occasionally cockney rhyming-slanged to a 'Michelle', as in Michelle Pfeiffer. Jamieson had a decent afternoon, taking two wickets for 23 runs, Davies took one for 19, while Anandanadarajah snaffled his wicket for 17 runs. The innings obviously ended on the bowling of Freedman, who only bowled 1.1 overs. Add up all the overs and you'll find they match the 12.1 that Rumpstead faced.

The only other thing to explain is how a win is calculated. This game is very simple. Both teams had their innings and Steeple Burpington scored 95 more runs, therefore winning by … erm … 95 runs. If – and given their scorecard this is a very, very big if – Rumpstead had managed to reach the target they would win in a different way. Let's say that they scored

187-6. They scored one more run than their opponents, but that doesn't really mean anything. The game ends after the delivery that puts them in front, so is there any difference between scoring 187, 188 or 189? Not really. Instead, the amount of wickets remaining is used to gauge the scale of the victory. In this case, they were 187-6, so they had four wickets remaining. They would have won by four wickets. They didn't, obviously, because they're rubbish. Especially that Macintosh character…

Extras

Being the astute type, you'll have noticed the presence of 'extras' on those scorecards. These are runs that have been credited to the batting side to punish the incompetence of the fielding side. Penalty runs, if you will. The higher the extras, the worse the fielding team has performed. They can also serve a dual purpose of embarrassing the batting team if they have under-performed. 'Blimey,' a horror-struck fan would say, 'Extras was our second highest scorer!' There are four flavours of extra, so let's have a look at them in more detail.

1. Wide

The bowler must always deliver a ball that the batsman has at least some chance of hitting. He can't cheat and bowl it so far away from his opponent that he can't get anywhere near it, otherwise a wide is awarded. A wide is a ball which is deemed by the umpire to be outside the reach of the batsman. This rather ambiguous definition changes according to the style of cricket. The umpires tend to be a lot harsher in limited overs cricket than in the longer form of the game and pointedly draconian in the Twenty20 games.

When a wide is awarded, a single run is credited to the batting side and will appear in the extras section marked as 'w'. If you've got a crafty streak then you're probably already imagining how this could work to your advantage. Imagine if your opponent needed to hit seven runs in the final over to win the game. The bowler could just bowl six wides and the game would be over! Ah, but no. Every wide ball is repeated. Bowl a wide and you'll be forced to bowl a seven-ball over. Bowl two wides and you'll end up bowling an eight-ball over. It's one of the more embarrassing things that can befall a bowler.

If a wide is so wide that the wicket-keeper can't stop it zipping off over the boundary behind the stumps then four

Fig. 5 The umpire signalling a wide

wides are awarded to the batting side. This is often the source of much hilarity to the batsman, although it doesn't mean that the bowler has to bowl four more deliveries. Just the one will do.

Wides can also be awarded for balls that bounce too high to be hit. Even if they go straight over the middle of the batsman's head, if they do it at an altitude of nine feet, it's not really very fair, is it? Bowl it again, silly.

2. No-ball

No-balls are the umpire's way of saying that the bowler is bowling unfairly. Like wides, they count as one run for the batting side and they must be bowled again. They are represented on the scorecard as 'nb'. There are three main varieties of no-balls:

1 The line in front of the stumps nearest the bowler is known as the 'popping crease' and the bowler must make sure that at least some part of his front foot is behind this line when he releases the ball. Failure to do so will mean that the ball is flung from too close a range.
2 The bowler must not throw the ball down the pitch by straightening the arm up just before release. This is known as 'chucking' and is frowned upon. There are a number of bowlers who have had suspect bowling actions, which have led to protracted and complicated tests from the cricketing authorities that we just haven't got time to go into. The general idea is simply to bowl it, not throw it.
3 The bowler must always inform the umpire if he wants to change the way that he is delivering the ball. The umpire can then let the batsman know and save him from a nasty, potentially painful surprise. This is usually just a change

from around the wicket bowling to over the wicket bowling or vice versa.

A batsman is under no obligation to play a no-ball, but if he does it can be very beneficial. Not only will he get to keep any runs on top of the penalty run, but the only way he can be dismissed is by a run-out. In theory this means that, at the shout of 'No-ball!', he can have a great big swing at it with impunity. A free hit. In some styles of cricket, Twenty20 for example, a no-ball can be followed by another free hit, a horrible double penalty for the bowler.

Fig. 6 The umpire signalling a no-ball

3. Byes

The batsman doesn't have to hit the ball to score runs for the team. If the ball whizzes past him and the wicket-keeper, he can run as if he had hit it. The runs won't count for him, though; they'll go down as byes, represented as 'b' on the scorecard. Byes are a sign that the wicket-keeper is either standing too close or that he's not very good. If a ball goes all the way to the boundary, it counts as four byes. As you can see from the picture below, the umpire signals byes by holding his hand up in the air, as if he's waving goodbye. Clever, innit?

Fig. 7 The umpire signalling a bye

4. Leg byes

If the batsman goes to play a shot, misses, and the ball bounces off his pads and away, he can still run. As long as he was either making an effort to play the ball, or even trying to get out of its way, it counts in the same way as byes. It doesn't go on his individual score, but it does go towards the team score, represented on the scorecard as 'lb'. Mind you, if the batsman is foolish enough to try and play the ball with his legs deliberately, a 'dead ball' will be called and no runs will be allowed. As always, if the ball bounces off the pads and away over the boundary, it's four leg byes.

Fig. 8 The umpire signalling a leg bye

Referrals

All things considered, it has to be said that umpires do an incredible job. Keeping focused for a whole day, unable to risk missing a thing, they still get far more decisions right than they ever do wrong. Unfortunately, every now and then, they do make mistakes and sometimes they can be very costly.

With this in mind, the ICC have been trialling a referral system in an effort to eliminate errors. England's tour to the West Indies in 2008 was the first time that it had been used in Test match cricket, but it won't be the last. In June 2009, the ICC decided to give the scheme another chance across international Test cricket, in spite of opposition from the ECB.

Essentially, the referral system is an opportunity to say to the umpire, 'I'm dreadfully sorry, old boy. I think you've got that one wrong.' Each team captain has two 'referrals' per innings. If there is a decision that he believes to be wrong, he can ask the third umpire, sat up in the stands, to review the television footage. If the captain is right and the umpire is wrong, the decision is reversed and he keeps his referrals. If the captain is wrong, he loses one and has just one left to use for the rest of the innings. When he's out of referrals, he must accept the umpire's decision on everything, no matter how ludicrous it seems.

The main problem, at least on the 2008 West Indies tour, was the amount of time that it took to go from the pitch to the third umpire and back again. Sometimes it could take ten minutes or so to get the game going again, which doesn't sound like much, but imagine if your team were chasing a target on the final day and it was getting dark. Every minute counts at that point. There was also the faint feeling that something wasn't right. Many cricket fans were uncomfortable with the concept of questioning the umpire's authority, as if it struck deeply into the heart of the game itself. If we were admitting that they could get things wrong, then were we opening up a precedent that would lead to their becoming obsolete? Why not just make every decision from the stands?

Averages

There are some who watch cricket for relaxation and there are some who like to see the slow development of a tactical battle. There are some who relish the big hitters and the fast bowlers and there are some who just love to see quality spin bowlers, sending their deliveries pirouetting down the pitch. Some people, however, watch cricket for a very different reason. They watch it because they just love numbers. Statisticians are a much-loved subculture of the cricketing family, mainly because most established fans have, at one time or another, kept their own scorecards and scribbled out the averages. Averages tell you everything you need to know about cricket players, which is why they are so jealously guarded. There are two kinds of average: a batting average and a bowling average. Let's start with the batting one, because it's probably the most simple.

The batting average

Imagine that you had played five one-day games of cricket. You'd had some good days and you'd had some bad days, but what kind of a batsman were you? In your first game, you'd racked up a nervous 19 before being dismissed. This was followed by a duck, a 5 and then you'd rallied a bit to score 34 and 52 in your last two matches. Tap these into the calculator and divide the total runs (110) with the amount of innings (5) and you'll have your average which is … 22.

Now, let's give you another innings on top of that, but let's say that you scored 40 without being dismissed. Not-outs are not counted as an innings when it comes to calculating your average. This means that you are now taking your total runs (150) and dividing by your total innings (still 5) to get a new average which is ... 30. You now look like a much better batsman. Generally, your typical international test batsman will have an average of about 40+, if that's anything to go by. It's important to remember that there is a difference between Test match averages and limited overs averages. In the shorter version of the game there are times when a batsman is forced to hit out quickly, sometimes sacrificing his wicket for the progress of the team. This rarely happens in the longer game, which is why batsmen always cherish these figures above any other.

Be warned though. Averages can give false readings. When I played for my school team it was only because they needed me to make up the numbers. In my first game I scored one. It was an appalling shot that went straight up in the air, but was somehow dropped by a fielder who was, it can only be presumed, my eager but useless equivalent at his own school. The next ball took my middle stump. After this display of ineptitude I was dumped down towards the back of the order, only coming in at the end of the innings. Here, in my natural habitat, I scored a 6 without being dismissed and then, astonishingly, 9 without being dismissed. My average, for this was the end of the season, was 16. I hadn't even come close to scoring 16 and yet it was my average. Always double check the amount of not-outs a batsman has accumulated.

In the limited overs variety of the game there are even more statistics to play with. Here, where time is at a premium, it's good to know how many balls a batsman needs to score runs.

If you were to face ten balls and score 5 runs, you would have a 50 per cent strike rate, which wouldn't be that good. If you were to face ten balls and score 15 runs, you would have a 150 per cent strike rate, which is much more like it. In Test matches, strike rates can drop down as far as 20 per cent; in Twenty20, they've been known to go as high as 250–300 per cent.

The bowling average

Bowlers have plenty of numbers to play with as well. The standard calculation for a bowler is how many wickets he can take for his runs. If you were bowling in a match and you took three wickets while giving away 66 runs, you'd have an average of 22 here. This would mean that you would cost your team 22 runs for every wicket you took, which isn't a bad rate at all. A bowler may take five wickets, which would be wonderful, but if he does it at the cost of 180 runs, then it's not that much use. His average would be 36. Not so good.

Bowlers also like to keep an eye on their economy. Sometimes they will take the number of runs that they have given away and divide them by the number of overs they have bowled. So, if you were to give away 50 runs in ten overs, you would have an efficiency of 5 runs per over. This tends to be used only in limited overs cricket and only by bowlers anxious to prove that, even though they haven't taken any wickets, this doesn't mean that they're rubbish. No siree.

Other factors

The weather

The weather, especially in the UK, is a huge factor in the outcome of any cricket match. While some nations can count on their summers maintaining a dry and summery kind of vibe throughout, this sceptered isle has a habit of attracting the most indecisive weather fronts in Europe. Sun turns to cloud and then to rain in a matter of hours, making a mockery of even the most well-prepared plans. Captains will keep a close eye on the weather, especially when deciding whether or not to bat or field first. If it's overcast on day one, but sunny thereafter, why not field first and then enjoy the sunshine? Here's what it all means.

Rain

You can't play in rain, no matter how wimpish you think it is to scuttle off to the pavilion at the first light pitter-patter. If you think it's difficult to face a 90mph ball in normal conditions, imagine doing it while blinking raindrops out of your eyes. Any kind of moisture on the pitch, as you'll see later, has a dramatic effect on the ability of the bowlers to get the ball to misbehave. Puddles would not be acceptable. When the rain comes, the game is suspended and the captains must adapt or face the prospect of a draw. Most teams will have a fair idea of the weather forecast, but there's no amount of preparation that can stop a complete washout. It's every fan's worst nightmare.

Cloud

The prospect of rain isn't the only thing that heavy cloud cover can bring. It will also put a smile on the face of any swing bowlers. The presence of moisture in the air can increase their ability to move the ball through the air, sometimes leading to the fabled 'reverse swing' that can send an offside ball arcing in at the leg stump. Big black clouds can also reduce visibility, which is not what you want when someone is hurling balls at you all day. If the light gets really bad, the umpire will ask the batsmen if they'd like to come off the pitch, in much the same way as they would if it rained.

Sun

There really is very little in this world more satisfying than being sat in a cricket stadium on a hot, sunny day, especially if you've managed to get seats near the bar. But it's not just the supporters who like the sunshine; the batting side will absolutely adore it. For starters, they can actually see the ball properly as it hurtles towards them. More importantly, it won't be hurtling towards them with quite the same regularity. Fast bowling takes a lot out of you, especially if you're doing it in near-Mediterranean temperatures, so long spells of bouncers are rather unlikely. Mind you, that's not so good for any batsman with a pathological fear of spinners. Fielders will suffer as well. Two and a half hours in direct sunlight, trotting backwards and forwards, occasionally breaking into a sudden sprint. That would sap anyone's concentration.

The pitch

You won't find many sports where the playing surface is under as much scrutiny as it is in cricket, but then there are not many sports where the surface is so integral to the game. A seasoned observer can usually wander up to the pitch, give it a quick look and then give you a good indication of how many runs will be scored and how long the game will last. It's all about the colour, the texture and the condition.

Colour
Green

If you can see patches of green in the wicket, then you know that there's going to be something there for the bowlers. The presence of little patches of grass may seem insignificant, but it's something for the ball to cling to when it pitches, potentially causing deviation in its flight path.

Brown

A brown, earthy pitch is good news for the batsman. It means that the ball won't alter its trajectory too violently. Most top level batsmen can deal with a straight ball, so the knowledge that pretty much everything they face will behave itself is a real security blanket to cling to.

Texture and condition
Wet

Ever wondered where the phrase 'a sticky wicket' has come from? It's here, on a wet pitch. Nowadays, with all the covers and protection that a pitch receives, it's actually very rare to encounter wet conditions, but it still happens if there is dew in the air in the morning, or if the groundsmen have been a little sluggish in getting into gear when it rains. Moisture on the pitch is a godsend for any spin bowler because, again, it's something for the ball to react to.

Dry

That isn't to say that a dry pitch favours a batsman. Although the first few sessions of a test match will be fairly predictable, it will eventually start to crack. Sunny weather exacerbates the problem, which is why the 'dustbowl' pitches of India and Pakistan can be so treacherous.

Soft

A soft pitch will absorb the power of even the fastest delivery, bringing 90mph balls down into the 80s, a huge difference at the top level of the game. A fearsomely paced bowling attack will have problems intimidating the quarry on a soft surface.

Hard

A nice, hard pitch, on the other hand, that's a different matter entirely. Suddenly, balls can rear up into the air at the batsman at a terrifying rate of knots. There is some compensation, though. A good, well-timed drive on a hard pitch can bring boundaries where perhaps it wouldn't on a different surface.

Cracks

Even in mild conditions, all cricket pitches will eventually start to age over the course of time. The constant pounding of bowlers' feet, of batsmen marking out their guard, of balls hammering down on the pitch – it all takes a toll. When cracks emerge on the playing surface, they shine out like a beacon to spin bowlers. Land a spinning ball on an imperfection and the effect can be devastating. Balls can veer off at hideous angles, confusing even the calmest batsman.

7

The competitions

International
The Test

For all of the excitement generated by limited overs cricket, there is nothing that comes even close to the majesty and primacy of Test cricket. With five days to play with, it really is less of a sport and more of a military campaign. Every factor, every aspect of cricket that we've discussed so far comes into play all at once. The captain of the team must deal with an inexhaustible supply of ever-changing parameters, as well as being constantly aware of his players and their abilities. If you ever get the chance to sit and immerse yourself in five days of cricket, I heartily recommend it.

Like all cricket matches, a Test match always starts with the toss of a coin. In this form of cricket, however, it's vital to make the right decision. If it's a sunny day and the pitch is flat and predictable, you can bet that both captains will want to bat first, set up a big score and then sit and wait. By the time the fourth innings of the match comes around, i.e. the fielding team's second innings, the pitch will have more cracks than the unluckiest man in the world's mirror. Because of the deterioration of the pitch, first innings scores tend to be higher than those accrued in the second innings.

Although most captains would prefer to bat first and avoid that nasty fourth innings, some of them will send their opponents in instead. It could be that the wicket is green, the first day is overcast and the weather is scheduled to improve, thus making the sunny second and third days the best time to score runs. A good knowledge of the weather forecast is absolutely vital.

There's also the state of the ball to worry about. A shiny, new ball is the tool of any fast bowler's trade, but it's no use to a spinner. For the first 20 overs or so, it retains its shape and shine, but then it slowly starts to bruise like old fruit. By the time it has seen 60 overs of service, the spin bowlers will be eyeing it greedily, like children outside a sweet shop window. A dented, roughed-up ball can be made to do all kinds of crazy things if it lands in the right way. The umpires will always offer a new ball to the fielding captain after 80 overs, though it should be said that he is under no obligation to take it.

Test matches are played in blocks of anything from two to five matches known as a 'Test series'. The objective is, obviously, to win more matches than your opponents, which can occasionally mean that teams will start playing purely to stop the other team from winning, by using too much time on their innings. That's another tactic that's generally frowned upon, but the important thing to remember is that Test series are played over a period of weeks and months with one specific aim in mind. Just when you were thinking that five days was a long time to play a game, eh?

Assuming that the weather holds out, Test matches should last for 90 overs a day, split into three divisions of play. In the

UK, the morning session tends to start at 11am before a lunch break at 1pm. At 1.45pm, the players return for the afternoon session which lasts until a tea break, usually at 3.45pm, before returning after half an hour for the evening session.

This final session is crucial. It can be played as the light deteriorates, or as established batsmen tire. Fielding teams will know that they are running out of time and will redouble their efforts. For this reason, it's not unheard of for a batting captain to respond to a dismissal by changing his batting order. Instead of sending out a valuable player who would be at risk of losing his wicket cheaply, they send out a weaker batsman, known as a 'nightwatchman'. His role will be simple. Don't get out. He won't try and score runs, he'll just block up and ease the team through the final session safely. Well, that's the idea anyway.

Batting in a Test match is a question of composure. There is so much time to sit and build up a good score, but the first moment of impatience can often be the last moment of an innings. The key is to hit runs at a steady rate, punishing the bad balls and blocking up against the good ones, always being ready for a surprise. Too much caution and the batsman will be compelled to start lashing out and that never ends well.

As we discussed earlier in the book, Test cricket is a very fine balancing act, which is why it's such a fascinating battle of nerves. Spend too much time batting and you won't have enough time to bowl. Try to bat too quickly and you'll lose wickets. Try to bowl too aggressively and you'll haemorrhage runs. The captain can declare at any time and end his team's innings, but sometimes that can be a silly move. You can't restart your innings later, so it means saying goodbye to any more runs. Mind you, if you delay too long before declaring, you can kiss goodbye to the chance of winning a game. A draw is no consolation when you know you should be celebrating a victory...

The Ashes

Of all the Test series in existence, the most prestigious is contested between England and Australia. 'The Ashes' take place roughly every 18 months, although because of the seasonal contrast from one hemisphere to another, there can be up to 36 months before the two nations meet.

The Ashes take their name from a peculiar episode way back in 1882 when Australia won their first Test in England, at the Oval in London. The English, who considered themselves the founders of the game, and therefore the superpower, were stunned to have been beaten by their own colony and, with typical British stoicism, they dealt with that humiliation with lashings of gallows humour.

'In Affectionate Remembrance of ENGLISH CRICKET,' read a mock obituary in the *Sporting Times*, 'which died at the Oval on 29th AUGUST, 1882, Deeply lamented by a large circle of sorrowing friends and acquaintances R.I.P. N.B. – The body will be cremated and the ashes taken to Australia.'

The English captain Ivo Bligh, suitably chastised, decided to use this little joke to spur his players on when they travelled to Australia the following season. He repeatedly told journalists that he would lead his side across the world to bring back those ashes and, as there's nothing a journalist likes more than being gifted a soundbite, the phrase quickly caught on. This wasn't about the cricket, it was about 'the ashes'.

Bligh was true to his word and, after leading England to victory, he was reportedly presented with a small terracotta urn by a group of well-to-do ladies. They told him that the urn contained the ashes of a cricket bail, symbolically burned to represent the demise of English cricket. The urn returned home with Bligh and remained in his possession until his death in 1927. His widow then gave it to the MCC and it became a part of their museum's permanent collection. Apart from a couple of very carefully arranged trips to Australia, it has remained there ever since, which is something of a surprise to anyone who thought that it was an actual trophy.

In fact, the urn has never been awarded to either side. It has always remained the property of the MCC, even in the face of public opinion. When Australia wiped the floor with England in 2002, there were calls for the urn to be transported Down Under until such time that its rightful owners could earn it back. A Waterford crystal replica was commissioned in 1998 to create a tangible trophy, but it doesn't seem to have changed anything. The two teams still seem happier to fight for the metaphorical possession of a very old, very small container of dust. And how they've fought. The Ashes can only be regained if the holders are beaten. A drawn series means that the holders simply retain the prize.

Over the years there have been some ferocious encounters, not least in 1932 when England captain Douglas Jardine hit upon a rather interesting tactic. He placed the bulk of his fielders on the leg side, ignored the stumps and ordered his fast bowlers to aim everything at the bodies of the Australian batsmen. Jardine gave his plan the rather bland name of 'leg theory', while the outraged and heavily bruised Australians bestowed on it the more sinister moniker of 'Bodyline'. Guess which name stuck? 'Only one side is here to play cricket,' complained the Australian manager. 'I haven't travelled 6,000 miles to make friends,' growled an unrepentent Jardine in response. 'I'm here to win the Ashes.'

A furious diplomatic row broke out and the MCC were eventually forced to change the rules to make sure it couldn't happen again. First they empowered the umpires to take action if they felt that the batsman's safety was being repeatedly compromised and then a limit was placed on the number of fielders allowed in the area behind square leg. This reduction of catching positions killed leg theory forever. Not that it's prevented the occasional bouncer being delivered…

Happier times were witnessed in 2005 when Australia travelled to the UK to defend the series against what most people believed was a weaker England side. The first Test didn't offer anything to change anybody's mind. England were battered, beaten by 239 runs having failed to breach the 200 mark in either innings. The second Test was a far closer affair. England set Australia a modest target of 280 runs to win the match, but began to work their way through the order with some certainty. Australia found themselves within two runs of victory, but down to their last wicket. Poor Brett Lee, a fine bowler, but a most unassuming batsman. He had worked so hard against the odds to secure the victory and he could only sink to his knees when his partner Mark Kazprowicz was dismissed. Andrew Flintoff had taken the match-winning wicket, but instead of celebrating he moved immediately to console Lee, a lovely moment that made everyone go all warm inside. A draw followed in the third Test before England found themselves in the rare position of asking their rivals to follow on in the fourth, a decision that eventually led to a narrower-than-they-would-have-liked victory. Leading the series 2-1 before the final Test at the

Oval, England only had to draw to regain the urn and, thanks to a heroic innings from Kevin Pietersen, that's exactly what they did. Cue nationwide celebrations and a quite phenomenal all-night bender from Flintoff, who managed to glug and burp his way through to the following afternoon. Now that's the kind of behaviour that made Britain Great.

One-day internationals (ODI)/Limited overs

The concept of limited overs cricket is actually relatively new. Mind you, in a sport as old as cricket, most things are. It wasn't until 1962 that the first competitive games were played at county level in the Midlands. The Gillette Cup, established in 1963, was the first full scale limited overs competiton. Teams would battle it out for what now seems like a whopping 65 overs.

But while the English established the style, others stepped in to convert it to the event it is today. Furious at missing out on the television rights to the Australian Test matches in 1976, media magnate Kerry Packer decided on a drastic course of action. If the Australian Cricket Board (ACB) were taking their ball and going home, that was just fine. Packer was taking the players. In 1977 he launched his World Series Cricket (WSC) upon an unsuspecting world, having spent the last year secretly signing up some of the world's best cricketers including more than half the Australian team and the England captain Tony Greig. And guess who got the TV rights to that? Yep.

For three awkward seasons, the spin-off sport challenged cricket on all fronts, but it turned into a gruelling war of attrition that neither side could afford. Eventually, the ACB caved in and gave Packer the TV rights he had wanted, ending the schism. But WSC left a great legacy. Floodlights, coloured kits and day/night games were all Packer's innovations. For the first time, cricket was presented as something more than a game. Now it was an all-round entertainment package, constructed for fans, both in the ground and on television.

Even before the advent of Twenty20 the limited overs game, particularly the ODIs, was the most profitable format. It's obviously far easier for most people to watch a single day of cricket, rather than a five-day stretch. Still fuelled by many of Packer's plans, the game attracts big crowds and huge television audiences, all of whom know that they'll be seeing a result, not a slow draw.

ODIs are 50-over affairs with a number of little tweaks to increase the excitement. For starters, no bowler can have more than ten overs, so the captains have to make important decisions about their attack. Do they use up the best bowlers on the best batsmen or do they play defensively with the swingers and bring on the pacemen to make mincemeat of the tail-end? When's the best time to use a spin bowler? Not against a batsman who makes a habit of slamming them over the boundary ropes, that's for sure. Timing is everything.

There are fielding restrictions to contend with as well. For the first ten overs of every game, there can be no more than two men placed outside of a 90-foot circle around the pitch. This encourages the batsmen to make the most of the opening exchanges because they should be able to hit the ball over the heads of the infield. Mind you, it's easier said than done. A brand new batsman facing a brand new ball may not want to start swinging out too quickly, especially as any mistakes will be greedily snapped up by that intimately placed cordon.

These periods of restrictions are known as 'powerplays' and there are two more of them in the innings. Both captains have to use one at some point before the 50 overs are up. The later powerplays only last for five overs each and the fielding team can have three players outside of the circle, not two. Powerplays can be played like jokers in a quiz night, at the request of either captain, but they do have to be used.

Batting teams will generally be looking to score runs at the rate of about one a ball to achieve a confident-looking score of 300, although 250 can often be enough to win a game. As always in cricket, it's all about balance. Play with too much aggression in the early stages and you run the risk of losing vital wickets.

As these games are much closer than Test matches, there are a number of proper draws where both teams score the same amount of runs. In ODI, if the totals are identical, the team that lost the least amount of wickets reaching it wins. If they still can't be split, then the game is tied. If the competition is at a knock-out stage and there absolutely has to be a result, a sudden death 'bowling-at-the-stumps' tie-breaker can be used. This is cricket's equivalent of a penalty shoot-out, where bowlers are forced to bowl at an empty wicket, but it's very rare indeed.

Duckworth-Lewis method

Now, if you thought that the lbw rule was a little tricky to get your head around, try this for size. Because the weather has a nasty habit of crippling limited overs games with the same cruelty as it damages Test matches, a system was required to make sure that a result could be always be achieved. The ICC had toyed with a hare-brained scheme called 'best scoring overs', but it was discredited in the 2002 World Cup after its implementation left South Africa requiring 22 runs from one ball. Up stepped a pair of English mathematicians, Frank Duckworth and Tony Lewis.

Using a system that treats remaining overs and wickets as 'resources', a published reference table can be used to calculate the amount of runs that a team 'should' be able to score. So, if a team should have 50 overs to score 300, but rain leaves them with only 30, a lowered target is set in place. The system isn't perfect. In the 2009 Twenty20 World Cup, England set the West Indies a target of 162 just before the rain set in. The Duckworth-Lewis method was used to calculate a new target of 80 runs in nine overs. It was still a challenge, but the West Indies had all ten wickets to play with, which meant that they could hit out without worrying too much about being dismissed. England, of course, had had to bat for 20 overs, being careful not to be so aggressive that they lost wickets early. The West Indies eased their way to victory.

That said, it's still the best method that anyone has managed to come up with and it does achieve the most important aim. Whatever happens, there will always be a result.

Net run rate (NRR)

In the group stages of limited overs tournaments, a net run rate is used to separate teams who finish on the same amount of points. This cricketing equivalent of 'goal difference' can be quite complicated to work out, especially over the course of a season, but thankfully you don't have to worry about that. The cricketing authorities have some outstanding statisticians on hand.

Put simply, a net run rate is the difference between the rate at which a team score their runs, set against the rate at which runs are scored against them. Hmmm, that wasn't very simple, was it? Ok, try this. If your team score 300 runs in 50 overs, you've scored those runs at a rate of 6 an over. If your opponents then bat for 50 overs and score 200 runs, their run rate is 4 an over. The net run rate for you is 2 (6 minus 4). Their net run rate is -2 (4 minus 6). See? That wasn't so bad, was it?

World Cup

As it is impossible to organise a Test match World Cup because of restrictions of time and weather, the most prestigious competition in international cricket is the ODI World Cup. First introduced in 1975, it is held every four years in venues around the world. The structure of the tournament changes almost every time, but it generally involves a seeded group stage and then a knock-out tournament which leads to a final.

Unfortunately, the 2007 World Cup was such a mess that the competition became something of a laughing stock. The initial group stages, instead of producing qualifiers for some exciting knock-out rounds, served only to feed another giant group stage of eight teams. These 'Super8s', as they were called, were nothing of the sort. The tournament rumbled on forever with day after day of 'dead' games between teams who were not able to qualify, eventually getting to the exciting bit just when most people had given up and switched off. The final, between Australia and Sri Lanka, ended in chaos as the Duckworth-Lewis method was used to find a winner, apparently without anyone telling the umpires. Throw in the facts that India and Pakistan, the best-supported teams, were dismissed in the first round, that the tickets were so expensive that no locals could afford them and that the stadium authorities banned anyone from bringing flags, horns or drinks, and it all adds up to a bloated, joyless procession of mediocre cricket.

If the World Cup is to retain its importance in the face of serious pressure from the Twenty20 game, it will need a heavy overhaul for future tournaments. There is room for both, but only if the ICC remember that they can't take the support of cricket fans for granted.

Twenty20

Ask any cricket fan what they make of Twenty20 cricket and you'll find two distinct camps: the traditionalists and the converts. Cricket, as you've seen earlier, is really supposed to be a cerebral challenge fought in a physical manner. Tactics should be vital, composure and calm should be integral. Twenty20 doesn't really go in for all of that and as a result, the traditionalists are not really that sure about it. Ignore them though, and join the converts. Twenty20 is the most exciting, absurd and utterly mental form of cricket that's ever been invented and it's the perfect way to get into the game. With such short innings, and rules painstakingly drawn up to punish time-wasting, no match lasts more than two and a half hours. This is a wonderful idea because, when you factor in half an hour before and half an hour after, that's exactly the amount of time it takes a grown man to get drunk. I wonder if that was intentional…

It's a simple game. Each team has 20 overs to score as many runs as possible. Over such a short period of time, there's not a lot of point in batting yourself in or preserving your wicket. It's all about the big hitters. If you even attempted to block a shot, your teammates would towel-slap you into oblivion in the showers afterwards. It's just not that kind of game.

It's very easy to tell how things are going in Twenty20. If no runs are scored from the delivery, it's a huge result for the bowler. This game is no friend to the bowlers and they'll be lucky to get more than five or six of these 'dot balls' every game. If one run is scored, it's still something of a victory for the fielding side. Any more than that and the batting team are laughing. Boundaries are at a premium, especially with the fielding restrictions in the powerplay during the opening six overs, when only two men are allowed to stand outside the 98-foot circle.

No bowler can deliver more than four overs in an innings and they are used carefully by the captain, who won't risk allowing a batsman to get used to a particular style. For those first six overs, you're likely to see a strong pace attack, with a spinner being used to slow things down when the fielding restrictions are lifted.

Teams will be looking to score runs at the rate of about eight or nine an over, which is more than one every delivery. That said, any score over 160 is potentially defendable. Twenty20 cricket is such a tight game that any team can beat any other team, something that can't always be said for the Test match version. Mistakes are costly, hesitation can be even worse. It's instinctive cricket for the thrill-seeking fan.

You don't need to know anything about the teams, the players or even the rules to understand Twenty20, which makes it the perfect gateway to the wider world of cricket. Ticket prices are still relatively reasonable, especially when compared to top flight football, so there's very little to lose by going down to your local county ground and taking in a game.

The atmosphere, boosted with loud music and gimmicks, is as electric as you'll find in cricket, although that may have more to do with the fact that the majority of the crowd are attempting to prove or disprove that three and a half hour theory we spoke about earlier.

Twenty20 World Cup

Even the conservative nay-sayers who had voted against its introduction could see that Twenty20 was going to be a part of the future of cricket. The swelling stadiums, and the equally swollen coffers, were evidence enough that they had stumbled across something of extraordinary value. And a sport of extraordinary value required a place on the global stage, every two years.

The first Twenty20 World Cup was held in South Africa in 2007 and was an intriguing affair, mainly because no one was entirely sure what they were doing or how seriously they should be taking it all. Tactics were few and far between, even by this shortened sport's own standards, and there were a few surprising results, not least the defeat of Australia by lowly Zimbabwe. The final was a marketing man's dream as it pitted India against their rivals Pakistan. The Indians set an impressive enough total of 157. Pakistan kept up with the run rate, but lost wickets at a worrying rate. They found themselves requiring 13 runs from the last over, a total that decreased sharply after a wide and a six. Unfortunately, the very next ball was walloped up in the air and taken by a fielder, ending Pakistan's challenge rather abruptly and sparking huge scenes of celebration across India.

Pakistan responded in the best possible way in 2009 in England, where they recovered from a shaky start to pick up momentum in the latter stages. South Africa were cast aside in the semi-finals before they eventually beat Sri Lanka at Lord's to lift the trophy. With huge viewing figures reported around the world, the 2009 tournament was conclusive proof that cricket had evolved into something more popular than ever before.

Domestic
County Championship

Unlike football and rugby, English cricket clubs are representative of their counties and not their towns. There are 18 county sides, which battle for four different competitions, the most important being the County Championship. Established in 1890, this is the Test match-style contest where each game lasts for four days.

For over a hundred years, the County Championship was one single division with every county playing the other one once, the venue changing from home to away with each year. But the ECB decided that there wasn't nearly enough excitement in an 18-team league with no relegation and just one winner, so in 2000 they rejigged it all. Now there are two divisions with a two-up, two-down system of promotion and relegation.

Because there are so many draws in this format of cricket, a special points system was introduced to incentivise teams against negative play. For the first innings of every game, bonus points are awarded for various milestones, but only up to 110 overs. They look like this:

200–249 runs: 1 point
250–299 runs: 2 points

300–349 runs:	3 points
350–399 runs:	4 points
400+ runs:	5 points

Then, when the batting team finish their innings, they get to bowl at their opponents with the following targets in mind. Remember, they only count for the first 110 overs.

3–5 wickets taken:	1 point
6–8 wickets taken:	2 points
9–10 wickets taken:	3 points

These bonus first innings points are added to the simple system of match-winning points below, which allows a team to win a game with anything from 14 to 24 points, making everything much more exciting.

Win:	16 points + bonus points
Tie:	7 points + bonus points
Draw:	3 points + bonus points
Loss:	Nothing but the bonus points

Unfortunately, none of this has done much to rescue the wider reputation of the competition. Despite the changes to the format, hot summers, promotional work and the success of the national team, there are still county games played out in front of double-figure crowds. The simple fact is that most people have jobs and these games tend to be played on weekdays. It doesn't help that the cricket clubs themselves continue to charge roughly the same for tickets as you would pay to see a half-decent gig in London. You can't help thinking that they could open the gates for free and make the same amount of money on selling refreshments, as well as opening the game up to the most important people of all, the future generation of fans, but I suppose they know best.

It's rather sad really because the county game is the breeding ground for the Test matches and the standard of talent on display is as high as it has ever been. Like Test matches, these games are an enthralling tactical battle of wits, but it just doesn't feel that way when you can hear your own applause bouncing off the backs of the empty stands. Regardless, if you want to watch some quality cricket at short notice, and you've got a day off work, you could do a lot worse than popping down to your local ground.

Twenty20 Cup

The Twenty20 Cup was the first competition of its type anywhere in the world and its popularity shook the very foundations of the sport. Games were scheduled for the early evening and played under floodlights, which meant that families could come along after work without missing a thing. The introduction of bursts of rock music to celebrate wickets and sixes, and other gimmicks like hot tubs, cash prizes for anyone brave enough to catch a six-hit, and even live appearances from pop stars, turned the traditionally sedate world of cricket into something approaching a carnival atmosphere.

Incredibly, it nearly didn't happen. The decision to experiment with the short game only passed with an 11-7 majority and even then there were a number of clubs who were rather dismissive of its prospects. They soon changed their minds in 2004 when a clash between Middlesex and

Surrey filled Lord's to the brim, the first time that a county game there had sold out since the 1950s.

Suitably convinced of T20's earning potential, the ECB moved to create a permanent league competition, replacing the old One Day league that had existed since 1969. The original concept was a grand affair with two overseas teams invited to join the fun, but these plans were downgraded rapidly after the Allen Stanford affair. Stanford, a Texan billionaire who hated Test matches but loved Twenty20, had wooed the ECB with a glamorous competition in the West Indies, luring English teams in with piles of money for cash prizes. In return, his team were set to join the new English Twenty20 league. It was a fantastic plan with only one minor drawback. Stanford, an international financier, had attracted the attention of the FBI. In February 2009, his offices were raided and in June he was arrested amid allegations of financial impropriety on a grand scale. That's the kind of thing that can really ruin a relationship with the English establishment.

The ECB have repeatedly tinkered with the format of the competition, trying to find the perfect balance between profit and excitement. As it stands, the 18 county teams are divided into two regional divisions, north and south. Teams play each other home and away with two points for a win, one for a tie or a no result and nothing at all for defeat. The top two from each division qualify for the semi-finals, with the winners meeting in a grand final.

Regional divisions in Twenty20

NORTH	SOUTH
• Derbyshire Phantoms	• Essex Eagles
• Durham Dynamos	• Glamorgan Dragons
• Leicestershire Foxes	• Gloucestershire Gladiators
• Lancashire Lightning	• Hampshire Hawks
• Northamptonshire Steelbacks	• Kent Spitfires
• Nottinghamshire Outlaws	• Middlesex Panthers
• Yorkshire Carnegie	• Somerset Sabres
• Warwickshire Bears	• Surrey Brown Caps
• Worcestershire Royals	• Sussex Sharks

As always with the Twenty20 game, it's all about the big-hitters. Many a journeyman county player has been transformed into a global star with a big innings, none more so than Essex's Graham Napier. In 2008, after a career that could best be described as modest, Napier wallopped 152 runs from just 58 balls, an astonishing innings that included 16 sixes and 10 fours. It was a knock that would eventually earn him more money than he ever could have expected in the English game because it attracted the attention of the Indian Premier League. More on them later...

If you're looking for a quick introduction to modern day cricket, the Twenty20 Cup is the best place to start. You'll get reasonable prices, ticket availability, local stadiums and all the action that anyone could ever ask for.

Pro40

In 1969, the ECB added a 'Sunday League' of ODI-style cricket to the domestic calendar, allowing clubs to attract an entirely new audience to the game. The Sunday League, which went under several names over the years, was originally a simple affair, much like the old-style County Championship. Every team played each other once during the season, on the Sunday that fell in between their First Class game. It meant that you could, for example, watch Essex against Warwickshire on Thursday, Friday and Saturday in the County Championship, Essex against Warwickshire on Sunday in the Sunday League and then watch the final day of the First Class game on Monday. Assuming, of course, that you had a very understanding boss.

That all changed in 1999 when the ECB split the division in two and introduced the concept of promotion and relegation, as well as spreading a number of Sunday games to other days. Unfortunately, in their infinite wisdom, the ECB also maintained a lengthy ODI-style cup with a complicated group stage. Throw the T20 and the County Championship into the equation and the resulting mishmash of competitions meant that, more often than not, the casual observer had absolutely no idea what was going on from one week to the next.

In 2010, it all changed one more time. The ODI Cup was dropped, the Sunday League was dropped and they were combined to form the Pro40. These games are 40 overs each, which means that batsmen have to be a little more disciplined than they are in T20. Three leagues of seven teams are all drawn from a hat at random. The 18 county sides are joined by Scotland, Ireland and an ECB Recreational XI. They play each other home and away with the group winners and the best second-placed team going through to the semi-finals. The winners of that go through to the grand final.

Indian Premier League (IPL)

If the English cricket authorities thought that they were tearing up the rulebook with their new Twenty20 competitions, they should have seen what was happening in India. Lalit Modi, the vice-president of the Indian Cricket Board, was busy sellotaping his rulebook to a missile and aiming it at the sun. Modi took a little longer, but when he unveiled the Indian Premier League he completely changed the face of the sport, turning cricketers into megastars.

The IPL is as close as cricket has ever got to the NFL in American Football or the English Premier League. It has three main themes: money, money and money. The IPL is dripping with cash. Players change hands in televised auctions, their salaries up for tender. Indian businessmen and film stars scrambled to acquire franchise rights to teams across the nation, before hurling out wages that the players themselves could barely believe. Suddenly it was possible to earn a career's worth of money in the space of one season.

Unsurprisingly, everyone wanted to get on board. The first season in 2008 took place with some of the biggest names in the game in attendance. The ECB, still unsure of the effects of this rogue element, counselled its players to steer clear, but by 2009, there was nothing anyone could do to stop them. Kevin Pietersen and Andrew Flintoff linked up with Adam Gilchrist, Matthew Hayden, Sachin Tendulkar and all the other members of cricket's glitterati.

Eight franchises were established for the first two seasons, although it is inevitable that more will join before long. They play each other home and away in a 14-game league season with the top four teams qualifying for the semi-finals. The winners of the league get to play the fourth-placed team, while second and third battle it out for the other place in the final.

The Board of Control for Cricket in India (BCCI) don't do things by halves. Every game is a jamboree of rock music, air horns and chanting, with the later balls receiving the same attention that a penalty might get in a football match. Dancing girls ring the stadiums, celebrating each six-hit with a combination of hip-wiggling and thrusting that would give the older members of the MCC an embolism. There are fireworks, big-screen TV replays and an awful lot of shouting. Somewhere underneath all of the madness, you might even hear the gentle thwack of leather on willow.

There are downsides though, the major one being that with so much money on offer, the IPL has actually endangered all other forms of the game. Why would you want to head to England to start the season on a chilly April morning in front of 26 people, when you could be in Calcutta being treated like a demi-god? The cricket authorities have had to work hard to ensure a compromise, but that doesn't come easy to these lumbering establishments. Thankfully, everyone now seems to have realised that fighting the IPL would be a waste of time, but the IPL have to remember that they need the longer form of the game to survive.

The stars of IPL made their names in Test cricket and they can only trade off them by continuing to play in the traditional competitions. There is room for the IPL within the greater sporting calendar, but only if both sides are capable of showing patience and understanding. Only time will tell if that's the case.

Women's cricket

Although it was only towards the end of the noughties that women's cricket began to force itself into the national consciousness, it has actually been in good health for over 250 years. The first recorded match was played in the summer of 1745, as you can see here from this magnificent bit of sports reporting in the Reading Mercury:

'The greatest cricket match that was played in this part of England was on Friday, the 26th of last month, on Gosden Common, near Guildford, between eleven maids of Bramley and eleven maids of Hambledon, all dressed in white. The Bramley maids had blue ribbons and the Hambledon maids red ribbons on their heads. The Bramley girls got 119 notches and the Hambledon girls 127. There was of bothe sexes the greatest number that ever was seen on such an occasion. The girls bowled, batted, ran and made catches as well as most men could do in that game.'

Thankfully, the game has come a long way since then. For starters, ribbons are no longer required. The structure of the game has been brought under the aegis of the ECB and, under the captaincy of Charlotte Edwards, this 'other' England won the World Cup in 2009. The increased media attention lifted the profile of the game to unprecedented levels, epitomised later that year when Claire Taylor was named as one of the Wisden Cricketers of the Year, the first woman to achieve such an accolade.

Thanks to the efforts of pioneers like the former England captain Rachael Heyhoe-Flint, the game has strengthened at all levels. Heyhoe-Flint led England to World Cup glory in 1973 after taking a leading role in the inception of the competition in the first place. She lobbied the MCC to allow female membership, which they eventually agreed to. There are now a number of domestic competitions, including Twenty20, limited overs and a County Championship, and Heyhoe-Flint herself has been recruited by the ECB to act as a consultant.

There are a lot of positives to women's cricket. The standard is excellent, the games are just as exciting, the ticket prices are cheaper, seats are more easily available, and then there's the most important factor of all: England are actually really, really good.

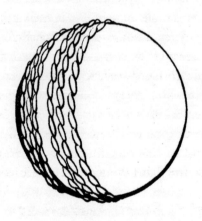

8

Cricket's best XI

Picking the greatest team of all time is fraught with danger. How can you judge a player of today's generation against one of, say, the 1930s? The simple answer is that you can't, but that won't stop people trying. Even with the benefits of averages and Internet footage there will always be a dispute as to the identity of the best of all time. My selection is no different. Who knows, if you really get into cricket now, perhaps you'll pick up this book and say, 'Eh? What's he picked Botham above Sobers for?' Secretly, I rather hope that's what actually happens.

Anyway, at the risk of offending and confusing, here is a team of cricketers that I think could take anyone at Test level.

Number 1, Sunil Gavaskar

You couldn't ask for a better opening batsman than Sunil Gavaskar, who represented India between 1971 and 1987. Calm and composed, he was an elegant stroke player who liked to take his time, keeping the scoreboard ticking over with gentle flicks and well-executed drives. He excelled against pace bowlers, especially the much-feared attack of the West Indies team of that era. Mind you, while he was a wonderful man to have in your team for a Test match, you wouldn't want him anywhere near you in a limited overs competition. Gavaskar didn't like to be rushed, as he proved in one 60-overs game when he carried his bat, surviving the entire innings but contributing just 35 runs. The match ended in controversy as fans stormed on to the pitch to vent their spleen at him. Still, we shouldn't let that get in the way of his 34 Test centuries, a record that survived for nearly 20 years before it was broken by his compatriot, who appears at number five in this team.

Number 2, Ricky Ponting*

He's been the bane of English cricket for years, but I'd still rather have Ricky Ponting with me than against me, even if he does look unnervingly like a young George W. Bush. Unlike the former president, however, Ponting is an excellent leader capable of inspiring the men around him and carrying a team to victory with the force of his own personality. The bitter sting of being the first Australian captain to lose a series to England in almost 20 years would have broken most men, but it only drove Ponting on. In the period that followed the Ashes defeat, Australia won 20 of their 21 Test matches and whitewashed England 5-0 in the next series. Ponting likes an aggressive shot, particularly a hook, and has scored more Test runs than any other Australian. He's also a phenomenal fielder with a fantastic record for instigating run-outs. English fans won't want to admit it, but he'd fit in this team quite nicely, thank you very much. He usually bats at number 3, but I've had to shift him up in the order because of this next chap...

Number 3, Sir Don Bradman

If you asked every single cricket fan on the planet to name their best XI of all time, there would be one unanimous choice and he's here as my number 3, Sir Don Bradman. The Australian was a prodigious talent, head and shoulders above anyone else on the planet. His prowess with the bat was one of the main reasons for England's decision to play 'Bodyline' in the Ashes of 1932. If they couldn't bowl him out, perhaps they could knock him out. After a career that stretched from 1928 to 1948, Bradman retired with a Test average of 99.94, a figure that no one else in history has come close to matching. Just read that again: 99.94. The next highest is Graeme Pollock with 60.97. Bradman would have ended up with an average of over a century if he'd just managed to score four runs in his final innings, but in a hideous moment of anticlimax, he was dismissed for a duck.

Number 4, Brian Lara

The only player in the team to have his own PlayStation game, Brian Lara was one of cricket's most exciting batsmen throughout the 1990s. He's still the only man ever to have scored a century, a double century, a triple century, a quadruple century and … erm … a … er … well, he scored over 500 runs as well. Lara made a habit of breaking records, including a whopping 375 and 400 not out against England and an extraordinary 501 not out against Durham at club level. Lara was a mercurial figure for the West Indies, just eclipsing his fellow countryman Sir Garfield Sobers on a number of occasions, although it took the influence of the legendary all-rounder to rescue his form. Sobers told Lara to alter his backswing after a dry spell; Lara obliged and the runs began to stack up again. An inspirational talisman for a team that, at times, flattered to deceive, Lara is the man any captain would call on to rescue an innings.

Number 5, Sachin Tendulkar

When you get down to number 5, you want a man who can steady the ship and score runs by the bucket load and there are not many better than the little master, Sachin Tendulkar. Don Bradman voted him into his all-time best team, Sunil Gavaskar said that he was as close to perfection as he'd ever seen and Shane Warne described him as the greatest player he'd played with or against, so at least we know he'd be popular with his teammates. He surpassed Brian Lara's all-time run scoring record in 2008 and holds all kinds of records for anything from the highest amount of centuries to the most centuries against Australia. Tendulkar is a glorious cricketer to watch. Only 5ft 5in, he could put the ball to the boundary with nothing but perfect execution, often scoring big hits with barely any follow through. We could do with a lad like him.

Number 6, Sir Ian Botham

Every good team needs a great all-rounder and the greatest of all time may very well be Sir Garfield Sobers. But I'm a sentimental fool and I've opted for Sir Ian Botham, a hero of my childhood and a cricketing legend. Botham was as adept with a bat as he was with a ball and had a habit of turning games around by force, most notably in the 1981 Headingly Test match against Australia. The visitors had scored 401 in their first innings, with Botham taking six wickets, but England could only respond with 174, 50 of which were scored by that man Botham. Forced to follow on, England struggled to make an impact until Botham arrived to score a rumbustious 149 not out before finally running out of partners. Set a target of just 129, the Australians were bowled out for just 111, with Graham Dilley taking eight wickets, an incredible achievement, but not enough to prevent the Test being forever associated with Botham.

Number 7, Adam Gilchrist+

It's very difficult to choose a wicket-keeper these days. Obviously, you want someone who can catch, but you also need a man who can score runs as well. In the all-time best team, there's only one choice for the perfect combination: Adam Gilchrist. The Australian 'keeper was so comfortable with the bat that he actually opened a number of innings. As far as style goes, he certainly wasn't the most refined character that the game has ever seen. He liked a big hit and was never afraid to slash out, whether it was a Test match or a one-day affair. Unsurprisingly, he was very popular in the Indian Premier League, taking over the captaincy of the Deccan Chargers in 2009 and leading them to the title, bagging the player of the series award at the same time. Gilchrist was another nightmare for the England team. Just when you thought you had the Australians on the run, up would pop Gilchrist for a barnstorming, match-saving innings.

Number 8, Shane Warne

To understand the importance of Shane Warne, you only ever need to watch one clip of footage. Just type 'ball of the century' into Google and you'll see what I mean. The ball pitches way out on the leg side and then, as if remote-controlled by a nefarious Australian in the stands, it veers wildly off course, whips past the bulky, static frame of Mike Gatting and takes the top off the off stump. And that was his first delivery on English soil. He got even better after that! Warne could make the ball do anything he liked and all the off-the-field attention in the world, of which he had plenty, meant nothing at all. He wasn't a bad batsman either. He never scored a Test century before his retirement in 2007, but he could usually be relied upon to come and stodge up the tail-end with an awkward 50. On top of all of that, he was a psychological nightmare to boot. Like most Australians, he had an acid tongue and loved to get inside batsmen's heads. Another one you'd rather play with than against.

Number 9, Malcolm Marshall

One of the most feared pace bowlers of all time, Marshall got an awful lot of speed and power from his relatively diminutive frame. At just 5ft 10in, he was still the scourge of the batting community from the mid 70s to the early 90s. Marshall died in 1999 at the ridiculously tender age of 41, but he packed a lot into his short life. One of the West Indies' 'Fearsome Foursome' of the late 1970s, he led a new generation of pace bowlers in the 80s when his career really peaked. He snared seven wickets for 22 runs in an innings at Trent Bridge in 1988 and took 376 in his entire Test career. His final average of one wicket every 20.95 runs tells its own story. Marshall could bat a bit as well, taking seven half-centuries in his test career at a time when bowlers were supposed to shuffle on, hit a couple of singles and then shuffle off again.

Number 10, Dennis Lillee

It doesn't matter who's in bat, nothing gives a man the wobbles like a really, really fast ball. For that, we can turn to Dennis Lillee, the terrifying Australian pace bowler who dedicated his life to making batsmen go twitchy. He bowled so fast that he gave himself spinal stress fractures, but he was so enthusiastic that he went into long-term physiotherapy and came back even stronger. Hugely popular with Australian fans, Lillee was a real showman who was roared into the wicket on every delivery. He ended his Test career in 1984 with averages of 23.92, having taken 355 Test match wickets. Blessed with stamina as well as pace, he was like a Duracell bunny, once putting so much into his action that his team lined up with a wicket-keeper and nine slips. Overkill, perhaps, but an important sign of how respected his bowling was.

Number 11, Muttiah Muralitharan

This Sri Lankan off spinner is the highest wicket-taker of all time, but he's a controversial choice. A strange bent-arm bowling action has meant that the bulk of his career has been spent under the spotlight as a succession of sports scientists try to ascertain whether or not he's chucking the ball. The consensus says no, but there will always be a small minority of people who want to doubt him. Never mind them though, he's coming on our team. Muttiah Muralitharan overtook Shane Warne's test record of wicket-taking, and averages around six wickets every Test match. It's all in his wrist. His super-flexible action allows him to move the ball on pitches that trouble other spinners and his 'Doosra', a ball that moves in the opposite way to his stock balls, is a potent weapon against batsmen. He might raise a few eyebrows for his bowling action, but he'll raise even more with the wickets he'll take.

Great stadiums of the world

Lord's Cricket Ground, England

The home of cricket remains one of the sport's most beautiful grounds, mixing traditional structures like the 19th-century pavilion with the crashed alien mothership of a press box, which won its architects a design award in 1999. Lord's is home to Middlesex County Cricket Club, as well as the MCC, and hosts cup finals and more than its fair share of Test matches. The creepy 'Old Father Time' weather vane can be spotted on top of the main grandstand, a macabre gift from Sir Herbert Baker in 1926.

Melbourne Cricket Ground, Australia

Known affectionately as 'the G' by locals, the Melbourne Cricket Ground (MCG) is a behemoth of a cricket stadium. With a capacity of just over 100,000, it makes Lord's look like a village ground. The MCG plays host to the traditional Boxing Day Test match, always played out to a full house of cricket-hungry fans. With the tallest floodlights of any stadium anywhere on earth, it's a daunting sight. Not bad for a venue that was first established in 1856 with a simple wooden grandstand.

DY Patil Stadium, India

Built in 2008, the DY Patil Stadium is one of the newest cricket venues in the world. Built to provide a home for the Mumbai Indians of the IPL, it has a capacity of 55,000. Every single fan receives an unobstructed view of the action thanks to the large cantilevered stands that surround the ground, negating the need for supporting pillars. The Patil Stadium played host to a world record-breaking century in its first season when Adam Gilchrist spanked a century from just 42 deliveries.

Newlands, South Africa

For aesthetic appeal alone, Newlands is in a league of its own. Overlooked by both the ominously named Devil's Peak, as well as the more sedately monikered Table Mountain, you could be forgiven for losing your wicket while you gazed happily at the view. Up until a recent redevelopment, fans could watch the game from large grass embankments up the sides of the field, but these have now been reduced by new stands, bringing capacity to 25,000, but limiting picnic opportunities.

Eden Gardens, India

Home to the magnificently named Kolkata Knight Riders, Eden Gardens is the largest cricket stadium in India. In fact, with a capacity of 90,000, it's only just outside the top twenty largest sports arenas in the world. The crowd at Eden Gardens are a vociferous lot and it used to be said that a cricketer's education was incomplete until he had played in front of a packed house there, a nice way of getting round the fact that riots are not exactly unknown in these parts.

Cricket conventions

A day out at the cricket is great fun, but there are still certain conventions that must be adhered to if everyone is going to have a good time. Stick to these dos and don'ts and you won't go far wrong. Ignore them at your peril.

Don't:

- Ask the batsman for his autograph as he returns to the pavilion. You'll have to go a long way to find a grumpier individual than a dismissed batsman. They're out either because they screwed up, or because the umpire made a mistake. Either way, the last thing they want to do is to scribble their name on your scorecard. Leave them alone to sulk.
- Get up out of your seat during the over. There's enough time at the end of every over for you to make it out of the stand, so don't rush it and prevent the people behind you from seeing anything. If you block their view of a wicket, you'll be so unpopular that you won't want to come back.
- Walk around behind the stumps when the game is in play. If you put off the batsman, he'll hold his hand up, the

game will stop and everyone will boo you. If it's a televised game, the cameras will pick you out within a matter of seconds, beaming your humiliation to everyone you know. Just wait until the end of the over.

■ Invade the pitch. It's not big, it's not clever and unless you're a naked woman of exceptional proportions, very few people will appreciate your intervention. The stewards will jump on you, you'll get dragged off the field and the police will probably want you to accompany them to the station.

■ Ask who's winning. This is the cardinal sin of all new cricket fans and it will mark you out as a know-nothing instantly. No one is 'winning' in cricket, teams just have sessions where they either do quite well or struggle. 'How are we doing?' is a far more appropriate question.

Do:

■ Make sure that you take the opportunity to wander around the ground. You'll find souvenir shops, bars, eateries and, at some grounds, museums. You're under no obligation to sit in your seat for the duration of the game, so take your time, stretch your legs and enjoy the day.

■ Check the restrictions on the sale of alcohol in the ground. Some competitions have complicated rules on when they can sell you beer and will close the bar for a couple of hours just when you decide that you'd like a drink.

■ Take suncream. A glorious day of sun-drenched cricket is a wonderful thing; getting so sunburned that your bare arms fuse themselves to the plastic seat is not. Bring the cream and slap it all over.

■ Check what you can and can't bring. Most county grounds will be quite happy for you to bring a cool box with sandwiches and grog, but there are some events where it will be confiscated as soon as you arrive. International fixtures are far stricter than domestic games, but make sure you do your research.

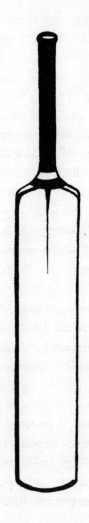

Sledging

Let's get one thing straight. Sledging isn't very nice. It is essentially the bullying of the batsman by the bowler, the wicket-keeper and the slip fielders. It's childish and pathetic that grown men can resort to calling each other names or attempting to put each other off, it's not a good example to set for younger players and, when it gets really nasty, it's morally repugnant. That said, it can be very funny. Here's some of the best sledging exchanges.

Australian Rod Marsh thought that it would be a good idea to goad Ian Botham as he made his way to the crease. 'How's your wife and my kids?' he shouted to England's best batsman.

'The wife's fine,' replied Botham calmly. 'The kids are retarded.'

Merv Hughes took great delight in mocking Robin Smith's attempts to get near his fast bowling in the 1989 Test match at Lord's. 'You can't f*cking bat!' he guffawed with typical Australian eloquence. Crack! Smith connected perfectly with the next delivery and sent it zipping off towards the boundary.

'Hey Merv!' *called* out Smith. 'We make a right pair, don't we? I can't f*cking bat and you can't f*cking bowl!'

But of course Merv *could* bowl, as this other episode shows. In a match against Pakistan, Hughes was a little out of shape. Well, ok, he was a lot out of shape. Javed Miandad went so far as to tell him so, informing the big Australian that he looked like 'a bus conductor'. Bad move. The very next ball blew his stumps to smithereens and Hughes charged past the dismissed batsman shouting, 'Tickets please! Tickets please!' at the top of his voice.

In fact, Big Merv caused batsmen so many problems that he used to have a stock of insults, pre-packed and ready for when he was short of time. 'Mate, if you turn the bat over and look at the other side, you'll find some instructions,' was one. 'I'll bowl you a f*cking piano, you Pommie poof, we'll see if you can play that,' was another. He really was a charming chap.

English legend Fred Truman could bowl as well, but he was horrified to find that his slip fielder, Raman Subba Row, couldn't catch. When the batsman edged Truman's delivery behind him it went straight through Row's legs. 'Sorry Fred,' apologised Row at the end of the over. 'I should have kept my legs together.'

'So should your mother,' snapped Truman.

Back in the 1930s, England captain Douglas Jardine, of Bodyline fame, was dismayed to hear his parentage being questioned by the slips. Outraged, he approached the Australian captain Bill Woodful and demanded an apology.

'Alright, you lot,' barked Woodful at his teammates. 'Which one of you b*stards called this b*stard a b*stard?'

Tubby spin legend Shane Warne used to love bowling at South African batsman Daryll Cullinan. The Australian took his wicket so often that Cullinan was known as his personal bunny. After a couple of seasons out with an injury, Warne welcomed him warmly back to Test cricket with an ominous 'I've waited two years to bowl at you again.'

'Yes,' replied Cullinan, 'and it looks like you spent it eating.'

Eddo Brannes was a bulky chap as well, something that Glenn McGrath was only too happy to point out. 'Oi Brannes,' he said during one encounter. 'Why are you so fat?'

'Because,' answered Brannes happily, 'every time I f*ck your wife she gives me a biscuit.'

But for a classier response, let's go all the way back to the days of Dr W. G. Grace for the final word. He had a terrible reputation for refusing to believe that he was ever out. In fact, in one match the ball took off one of his bails and knocked it to the ground, but undaunted Grace bent down, picked up the bail and put it back on the stumps. 'Twas the wind which took thy bail off, good sir,' he said to the umpire.

'Indeed,' replied the official. 'Let us hope thy wind helps the good doctor on his voyage back to the pavilion.'

Glossary

All out When a team have lost ten wickets they are all out. Their innings is over and it's time for the next team to come in and bat.

All-rounder A player so innately talented that he can be relied upon to bat with as much success as he bowls. Genuine all-rounders are quite rare, but a good one, like Sir Ian Botham or Andrew Flintoff, can make a huge difference to the prospects of any team.

Appeal The big shout that goes up when the fielding team believe that they have taken a wicket. They are appealing to the umpire to confirm whether or not he thinks they are right.

Around the wicket A ball bowled with the hand of the bowler furthest away from the stumps. Around the wicket bowling increases the angle of attack, so it can make catches and lbws more likely.

The Ashes The name given to any Test series between England and Australia.

Averages Statistics used to measure the average performance of batsmen and bowlers. Batsmen like nothing more than to have a good-looking average score and they get very upset if it is ruined.

Bad light When it gets so overcast and gloomy that it's actually quite difficult for the batsman to see the ball. The umpires will 'offer the light', which gives the batting team the chance to go inside and wait for things to brighten up.

Bails The little bits of wood on top of the stumps. There are two of them and if either one is knocked off the stumps by anything other than the wind, the batsman is out.

Ball The little red sphere that bowlers hurl at batsmen. Also, another way of describing a delivery, i.e. three balls left of the over.

Barmy Army The booze-soaked, sunburned collection of supporters who follow England around the world, drinking and singing all the way. The name stuck after a notable period of English incompetence in the mid 90s when independent observers struggled to understand the sanity of people who spent so much money watching such a hopeless team.

Bat 1. –n. The lump of wood that you use to hit the ball.
2. –v. To strike at the ball with the bat.

Bodyline 1930s' England captain Douglas Jardine's idea of bowling the ball directly at the batsman and positioning all of his fielders on the leg side in the hope that the ball would bounce off towards them.

Bouncer A fast ball that pitches short and goes straight up, usually at the batsman's head.

Boundary 1. The line that marks the edge of the playing area.
2. A shot that hits or goes over the rope.

Bowl To deliver the ball towards the batsman.

Bunny A bowler who is so bad at batting that anything he hits is a bonus.

Bye Run awarded when the batsman hasn't hit the ball, but has run anyway.

Caught To be dismissed by hitting the ball into the air and having it caught by a fielder.

Caught and bowled To be dismissed by hitting the ball in the air straight back to the bowler. Always embarrassing for the batsman.

Caught behind A batsman who makes the slightest contact with the ball, but sends it behind him for the wicket-keeper to catch, has been caught behind. It usually happens when nervous batsmen go to hit the ball and then pull away too late, catching a distinct and fatal edge.

Century If a batsman is good enough to score 100 runs then he has achieved a century. All batsmen aspire to this.

Chinaman A chinaman is the strange name given to a ball from a left-arm spinner which zips off in the opposite direction to that which was expected, into the batsman instead of away from him. A very rare form of bowling, it most likely took its name from its first practitioner, Ellis Achong, a West Indian of Chinese descent.

Chucking To be labelled a chucker is to be called a bounder, a cad, a cheat and a swine. In cricket, the ball is bowled, not thrown. Chuckers are frowned upon.

Clean-bowled When a bowler beats a batsman so convincingly that he cannot get his bat anywhere near the ball before it shatters his stumps, he has been clean-bowled.

Collapse Sometimes two batsmen can score runs with impunity for hours, but the moment that one of them is dismissed, everyone gets dismissed. A collapse is the dramatic sight of a previously impressive innings suddenly going to the dogs without reason. Wherever you see a string of single-figure scores in a batting scorecard, you see the evidence of a collapse.

County Championship The two-tiered domestic first-class league, in existence since 1890. This is the breeding ground of Test cricket and the competition is the most prestigious at domestic level.

Covers 1. A fielding position to the batsman's off side, relatively near and about halfway along the pitch.
2. The big heavy things that get pushed on to the pitch when it rains.

Cracks When the pitch starts to break up towards the end of the game, the spin bowlers are delighted. They can aim the ball at the cracks in the ground and get more movement.

Crease The crease is the white line just in front of the stumps. It marks where a batsman can and can't be stumped and where he must ground his bat to avoid being run out. Another crease, at the non-striker's end, marks where the batsman must ground his bat to score a run. Assuming his partner does the same at his end, obviously.

Day-night game A day-night game is a match that starts in the afternoon and finishes after it has got dark, the final stages being played under bright floodlights. Day-night games are popular with the fans because they can be fitted in around work and families.

Declare When the batting captain decides that he has batted long enough, he can end the innings by declaring.

Deep A fielding position prefix that indicates a place quite far away from the stumps, like deep square leg.

Delivery Another way of describing a ball from a bowler, e.g. 'Gosh! That was a bloody quick delivery!'

Dismissal When a batsman is out.

Doosra A ball that goes from leg to off when you were expecting it to go from off to leg.

Dot ball If a ball is bowled and nothing happens – no runs, no wicket, no extras, no nothing – then it is a dot ball, so called because it will be represented on a professional scorecard with a simple dot.

Draw When two teams are unable to forge a result in a two-innings, Test match-style game, then the match is deemed to be a draw. This is not the same as a tie, where both teams score the same amount of runs.

Duck To be dismissed without scoring a run. A very sad moment for any batsman, although not as sad as a 'golden duck' (see below).

Duckworth-Lewis A complicated way of determining results for games affected by the weather.

The England and Wales Cricket Board (ECB) The governing body of cricket in the UK.

Economy The name given to the rate at which runs are scored from a bowler's bowling. Bowlers like to be as inexpensive as possible. If a bowler has had 10 runs scored in his five overs, he has an economy of 2, because on average he is giving away 2 runs an over.

Edge To get the slightest of touches on the ball from the edge of the bat. Edges can be either very useful, sending the ball veering off at an unexpected angle to an empty section of the pitch, or very dangerous, directing it instead to the grateful hands of the wicket-keeper.

Extras The runs awarded to the batting team for fielding (byes and leg byes) and bowling (wides and no-balls) errors.

Fall of wicket (FOW on scorecard) The area on a scorecard which tells you when the wickets fell. If the score suddenly changes from 25-0 to 25-1, then the first number will be 25. A movement from 25 to 50 before the second wicket would give you a FOW of '25, 50'. The FOW is a useful way of finding out how a team progressed through their innings and when the trouble started, if indeed it did at all.

Field The area of grass where the game is played, usually a 500-foot circle.

Fielder One of the bowling team, but not the bowler and not the wicket-keeper.

Fine A fielding position prefix that indicates a place behind the batsman.

First-class A way of describing the longer version of the game at domestic level, i.e. the County Championship.

Five-for (fifer) Any bowler good enough to take five wickets in a single innings has achieved a 'five-for'. Its name originates from the bowling figures which, had he given away 40 runs, would read 'five for forty'.

Flannels The colloquial name given to the cricketers' white attire.

Follow-on If the second team to bat are really hopeless and finish more than 200 runs behind their target, the first team can insist that they stay out there and follow their first innings with their second innings.

Four Four runs are scored if the ball is hit and passes over the boundary rope, after touching the ground.

Golden duck A duck inflicted on a batsman's first ball.

Googly A ball that should bounce from leg to off, but goes from off to leg instead.

W. G. Grace Enormous cricketer of yesteryear with a dirty grey beard and a habit of disputing decisions. A legendary player, but a bit of a diva.

Gully A fielding position at a right angle to the batsman on the off side and slightly rearward.

Hat-trick If a bowler can dismiss three successive batsmen with three successive balls, then he has achieved a 'hat-trick'. The feat is so named after the now-defunct tradition of the team having a whip-round and buying the protagonist a hat to say 'well done'. It is a tradition that needs to be revived. There aren't nearly enough hats on men these days.

Hawkeye Hawkeye is the name of the technology used by TV stations to judge the flight of the ball. It is now used by the third umpire to help him reach lbw decisions in the instance of a referral.

Howzat The universal cry of any bowler or fielder appealing for an lbw or a catch behind.

International Cricket Council (ICC) The governing body of world cricket.

Indian Premier League (IPL) The glamorous, big-bucks Twenty20 league in India, where the game's top players command enormous salaries.

Infield The area of the field nearest to the batsmen.

Innings 1. The name given to the batting team's turn to bat, i.e. 'England's first innings'.
2. The name given to the batsman's go, i.e. 'Macintosh needs a good innings'.

Innings victory Any team that can achieve victory in a two-innings game after only needing to bat once has won by an innings.

Interval In limited overs cricket, the interval refers to the short break between innings. In two-innings cricket, it can mean lunch or tea.

Leg before wicket (lbw) The rule that prevents a batsman from putting his leg in front of the stumps to block the ball.

Leave To allow a ball to pass you without making an attempt to hit it. Not a good idea when it's heading for the stumps.

Leg 1. The on side of the batsman.

2. A fielding position prefix that indicates a place on the leg side.

3. One of a matching pair of limbs between a chap's bum and his feet.

Leg bye Runs awarded for running after the ball has hit the pad.

Line and length Essentially, line and length is a reference to the aiming axis of any bowler. A good length would see the ball bouncing at about bail height, a good line would mean that it would hit the top of the off stump.

Lord's Cricket Ground A large cricket stadium in north London, generally regarded as being the home of the game.

Maiden When an over passes without a single run being scored. Maiden overs are much cherished by bowlers and are always rewarded with a round of polite applause.

Marylebone Cricket Club (MCC) The MCC is a private members' club based at Lord's. They own the laws to the game and, before the rise of the ICC, they were entrusted with looking after its future. Members wear rhubarb and custard coloured ties and occasionally fall asleep in the middle of the afternoon session.

Mid A fielding position prefix that indicates a place roughly in the middle of the field.

Middle (to be out in the middle) The 'middle' is a reference to the batting strip. If you spend a lot of time in the middle, then it means that you bat for a long time without being dismissed.

Minor counties The county sides, like Hertfordshire, outside the professional game.

Net run rate (NRR) The rate of runs scored by you minus the rate of runs scored against you. A complicated form of 'goal difference' used to separate teams in group stages and leagues.

Nets Batsmen practise their art in small netted enclosures, with bowlers hurling down a succession of balls for them to try to hit. If a batsman is told that he needs to spend more time 'in nets' it means that he needs some practice.

New ball Every new innings starts with a nice shiny new ball. Fast bowlers like a new ball, but spin bowlers prefer to use an older one. After a set number of overs, usually 80, an old ball can be replaced with a new one.

Nightwatchman Rather than sending a good batsman into a gloomy encounter with the fast bowlers, some captains will prefer to send in a bowler to bat and tell him to shut up shop for the evening. It minimises the chance of losing an important wicket in nasty conditions. These brave blockers are known as 'nightwatchmen'.

No-ball When the bowler delivers a ball incorrectly, either by stepping over the line of the crease, throwing or not informing the umpire of a change in style.

Non-striker's end The stumps that a batsman stands next to when he isn't facing the bowler.

Not out When a batsman has survived his team's innings without being dismissed. Because you cannot have just one batsman, there is always at least one 'not-out' in every innings.

Off The bat side of the batsman.

On The leg side of the batsman.

One-day cricket Any form of limited overs cricket, completed in one day.

One-day international (ODI) The standard version of the limited overs game where two international teams bat for 50 overs each.

Openers The first batsmen on the pitch, numbers 1 and 2 in the order.

Order The order in which the batsmen come into play. Top order batsmen are usually the best; lower order are the worst.

Out When a batsman is dismissed.

Outfield The area of the pitch nearest the stands, where fielders stand and scratch their bottoms.

The Oval Cricket stadium in south London, home to Surrey and the site of the famous Australian victory that started off the whole Ashes episode.

Over Bowlers can only bowl in six-ball sessions, known as 'overs'. After the sixth ball, the umpire shouts 'Over!' and everyone shuffles around while a new bowler comes in and begins his over.

Over the wicket A ball bowled with the hand of the bowler that is nearest to the stumps. Over the wicket bowling narrows the angle of attack.

Pads The big cushions that you strap to your legs to prevent injury.

Pad up The signal given to a batsman to indicate that he should put his protective clothing on. Most batsmen pad up when they're two wickets away from going in.

Pavilion The big white building on the side of the pitch where the changing rooms are and where the batsman sit while they wait to go in. Any dismissed batsmen are said to be heading back to the pavilion.

Pitch 1. The pitch is the 22-yard strip of very, very short grass where all the action takes place.

2. The point where the ball hits the ... erm ... pitch.

Popping crease The name of the crease that runs just in front of the stumps. Its name comes from the very early days of cricket when a batsman had to pop his bat into a hole behind the crease for a run to count, while the fielders had to pop the ball into the same hole to run them out.

Powerplay A period of fielding restrictions that limit the amount of men in the outfield. The concentration of fielders inside the inner circle means that batsmen can go for big hits, but it also means that any mistakes will be punished.

Pyjamas The colloquial name given to the coloured clothing that players wear in one-day games.

Rain Horrible wet stuff that brings an abrupt end to any cricket.

Referral The trialled system of using TV replays to confirm umpires' decisions.

Rope The boundary of the field which can be marked out in rope or paint or by cushioned mini-advertising hoardings.

Run The currency of cricket. A run is scored when the batsmen run and ground their bats at the other end of the pitch.

Run rate The amount of runs that are scored every over on average. Scoring 40 runs in ten overs would be a run rate of 4 an over.

Run out If the fielder returns the ball to the stumps before the batsman can ground his bat past the crease, then he's been run out.

Runner If a batsman is immobilised by injury, he can call for a runner to help him out. The injured man must still play the shots, but he can stay still while his teammate does all of the leg-work.

Scorecard Big sheet of paper with all of the numbers on. You can usually pick them up at the stadium on your way in.

Scorer The man who compiles the official scores and transfers them to the scoreboard. These days there are teams of scorers, but in the old days it was two old men with a lot of sandwiches.

Seamer A fast bowler who tries to land the ball on the seam in order to make it change direction.

Series A run of games between two countries, like a five-match Test series.

Session A period of play broken up by a lunch break, a tea break or the end of the day. There are three sessions in every day of cricket.

Sight screen The big white constructions on wheels that stand at either end of the pitch. The sight screen blocks out the contrasting colours of the stadium or crowd, replacing them with a nice white block upon which the red ball is clearly visible. Games played with a white ball have black sight screens. Woe betide a chap who walks in front of the sight screen during the game.

Silly A fielding position prefix that indicates that the fielder is too silly to realise that standing right next to the batsman is a really good way to get hurt.

Single When one run is scored it is known as a 'single'.

Six When the ball is walloped high into the air and passes over the boundary rope without hitting the ground, a six is scored.

Sledging The trash talk exchanged by batsmen and fielders.

Slip Slip fielders stand alongside the wicket-keeper looking for little edges off the bat. The nearest slip to the 'keeper is called the first slip, then the second and the third and so on and so forth.

Spin A style of bowling that relies more on the movement of the ball after pitching, than on pace. Spin bowlers are slow but deadly.

Square leg A fielding position at a 90-degree angle to the batsman down his leg side.

Striker's end The stumps where the batsman stands as he prepares to face a delivery.

Stumped To sneak out of your crease, miss the ball and then hear the tell-tale clunk of the wicket-keeper knocking your stumps off. A very embarrassing way to be dismissed.

Stumps 1. The wooden sticks in the ground that make up the 'wicket'. There is an off stump, a leg stump and a middle stump.

2. The end of a day's play. 'That's stumps, lads. Whose turn is it to make the tea?'

Sundries A posh word for 'extras'.

Sweeper A defensive fielding position, backward of cover or midwicket and used primarily to prevent fours.

Swing The movement of the ball in mid-air made possible by mind-boggling aerodynamics.

Tail-end The bottom of the batting order, where the bowlers lurk. Tail-enders are very rarely any good with a bat.

Tea An afternoon break, usually taken at around 4pm.

Test match The engaging five-day battle between two international cricket teams.

Third man A fielding position behind the stumps on the off side and quite near the boundary. Like a really, really backward slip.

Throwing *See* Chucking.

Tie A genuine draw, when both teams score the same amount of runs and share the points.

Tonking Hitting the ball really, really hard.

Total The total number of runs scored by a team at the end of an innings.

Tour The name given to a visit made by an international team. Tours can include Test matches, ODIs, Twenty20s and games against domestic sides.

Twelfth man Teams are allowed a twelfth man to act in an auxiliary role. Usually, he'll bring out drinks or replacement equipment, although he'll normally combine that with bringing instructions from the captain in the pavilion. If there is an injury to a player, he can act as a substitute fielder, but not as a batsman or a bowler.

Twenty20 The shortened version of the limited overs game where teams bat for 20 overs each.

Twenty20 World Cup The international tournament for the shortened game, in existence since 2007.

Umpire The game's official. There are two umpires on the pitch, one at the bowler's end and another at square leg. In the big games, a third one sits in the stands to judge televisual replays.

Urn The tiny container that is believed to hold the ashes of a 19th-century bail.

Walk The act of leaving the middle after a dismissal. Any gentleman worth his salt will always know when he is out and will walk without waiting to see the umpire's finger, but the world is full of scoundrels willing to abuse this unspoken rule.

Wicket A tricky one this, it can mean a number of things.

1. If the batsman is in, he has kept his wicket. If he is out, he has lost his wicket. If a bowler bowled him, he took his wicket. If a team is, for example, 150-4, they have six wickets left. To give it a vulgar twist, a wicket is like one of the team's 'lives'.

2. The 22-yard pitch. A sticky wicket is a wet pitch; a lovely wicket is a flat pitch.

3. The stumps, as in 'he hit his own wicket'.

Wicket-keeper The man behind the stumps with the big gloves and pads. Represented with '+' on scorecards, he'll be there to take catches or stump the batsman.

Wide When the bowler bowls the ball so far wide that the batsman can't realistically be expected to hit it. Punished with a penalty run and an extra ball.

Wisden The colloquial name of the *Wisden Cricketer's Almanack*, the longest-running sports annual in the world. *Wisden* was first published in 1864, and there's been one every year since then. Easy to recognise, they're printed in bright yellow covers and, packed with facts, figures and records, are thought of as something of a cricketing bible.

World Cup The leading ODI competition, in existence since 1975.

Yorker A fast ball that pitches right at the batsman's feet, taking him by surprise. Yorkers are the complete opposite of bouncers.

Index

Also available:

Everything You Ever Wanted to
Know About Golf But Were
too Afraid to Ask

ISBN: 9781408114971

Everything You Ever Wanted to
Know About Football But Were
too Afraid to Ask

ISBN: 9781408114964

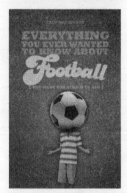

Everything You Ever Wanted to
Know About Rugby But Were
too Afraid to Ask

ISBN: 9781408114940